Empowerment Starts Here

Seven Principles to Empowering Urban Youth

Angela Dye

ROWMAN & LITTLEFIELD EDUCATION
A division of
ROWMAN & LITTLEFIELD PUBLISHERS, INC.
Lanham • New York • Toronto • Plymouth, UK

Published by Rowman & Littlefield Education
A division of Rowman & Littlefield Publishers, Inc.
A wholly owned subsidiary of The Rowman & Littlefield Publishing Group, Inc.
4501 Forbes Boulevard, Suite 200, Lanham, Maryland 20706
www.rowmaneducation.com

Estover Road, Plymouth PL6 7PY, United Kingdom

British Library Cataloguing in Publication Information Available

Library of Congress Cataloging-in-Publication Data

Dye, Angela.
Empowerment starts here : seven principles to empowering urban youth / Angela Dye.
p. cm.
Summary: "This book provides insight on how educators can increase the efficacy and achievement
of urban youth. Angela Dye shares instructional methodologies and stories to help the reader develop
an intimate understanding of the empowerment principles in action. Through these principles and
methods, individuals can increase their capacity to combat the psychological, social, and political
challenges associated with student achievement and real school reform" —Provided by publisher.
ISBN 978-1-61048-581-4 (cloth : alk. paper)—ISBN 978-1-61048-582-1 (pbk. : alk. paper)—ISBN
978-1-61048-583-8 (electronic)
1. Education, Urban—United States. 2. Education, Urban—Social aspects—United States. 3. Children with social disabilities—Education—Social aspects—United States. 4. Academic achievement—United States. 5. Educational change—United States. I. Title.
LC5131.D94 2012
370.9173'2—dc23
2011036899

♾️™ The paper used in this publication meets the minimum requirements of American
National Standard for Information Sciences Permanence of Paper for Printed Library
Materials, ANSI/NISO Z39.48-1992.

Printed in the United States of America

Granny
My Safe Harbor
Earth, Wind, and Fire
All Wrapped into One

This book is dedicated to you.

Contents

Empowerment Framework and Definitions

Statement of Empowerment
Empowerment is the power that one has to produce, to prosper, and to promote growth in self and in others.

Philosophy of Empowerment
The philosophy of empowerment is grounded in the premise of self-actualization. When one self-actualizes, he becomes his best self by reaching his highest place of being (in the physical sense of human living). In this place, he is able to produce, prosper, and promote growth in self and in others.

Definition of the 3 Ps: Production, Prosperity, and Promotional Growth
Production is the producing of outcomes by way of using one's skills, talents, and resources; prosperity is a state of being that relates to success (however one defines success); and promotional growth is the ability to inspire personal growth in self and in others.

Activating Principles of Empowerment
In order for a person to self-actualize to produce, prosper, and promote growth, seven empowerment principles must be activated.

- P^3 commitment
- Innate power
- Personal assets
- Global efficacy
- Individual responsibility
- Sense of self
- Shared authority

Instructional Framework to Empowerment
"Empowerment" is the instructional approach to teaching students how to use power to achieve a life of production, prosperity, and promotional growth. In an empowerment-based environment, all seven principles must be activated, aimed for, and highly regarded.

Key for Acronyms, Principles, and Program Names

Core Instruction
Core Instruction is a teacher directed program (a component of SBC programming).

GLC7: Global Leadership Curriculum
Global Leadership Curriculum (GLC7) is a seven-step project-based learning program (a component of SBC programming).

Global Efficacy (Empowerment Principle 4)
Power is related to a person's worldly presence and his ability to leave a legacy. Going beyond the impact that others have had on the individual, power is in the impact that the individual has on the world around him.

Individual Responsibility (Empowerment Principle 5)
Power is related to the successful fulfillment of one's social roles. This fulfillment generates a level of respect from others, allowing the individual to use this respect, and its treatment, as a power source.

Innate Power (Empowerment Principle 2)
Power is related to a person's natural right (and responsibility) for voice, choice, and dominion. In using one's voice, choice, and dominion, the individual understands how power is used to produce results. Through these actions, power becomes personal.

Institute
Institute is an orientation and assessment program (a component of SBC programming).

LASSS: Leadership in Action: Self, School, and Society
Leadership in Action: Self, School, and Society (LASSS) is a service learning program (a component of SBC programming).

P³ Advisory
P³ Advisory is an advising and accountability program that promotes students' disposition for production, prosperity, and promotional growth (a component of SBC programming).

P³ Commitment (Empowerment Principle 1)
Power is related to the personal commitment and drive one has to produce, prosper, and promote growth. The thoughts, beliefs, and attitudes one uses in order to self-actualize generate energy that can ultimately be used as a source of power.

PSGL: Preparatory School for Global Leadership
PSGL was the first school that used the SBC–Empowerment Program.

Personal Assets (Empowerment Principle 3)
Power is related to what a person can do and what he has. Divided into three categories: Internal Resources (skills and concepts related to reading, writing, math, science, and social studies); External Resources (technology, time, money, and human labor); and Interpersonal Resources (analysis, autonomy, valuing, communication, and collaboration), personal assets can be manipulated as power sources.

SBC: Social Being and Change Operations and Programming
SBC is an empowerment-based program for teaching, learning, leadership, and school management.

Sense of Self (Empowerment Principle 6)
Power is related to the control that one exerts over self while minimizing the control that others have over his person. Through five dominions, the individual does not wait for others to give him personal meaning. He assigns it to himself. As a result, the individual is liberated from the whims of others and can protect self from unhealthy relationships and unproductive situations.

Shared Accountability (Empowerment Principle 7)
Power is related to the ability to collectively produce, prosper, and promote growth. Through this shared experience, objectives are proactively established, allowing the individual to hold himself accountable to the outcomes of those objectives.

SSLP: Standardized Staff Leadership Program
Standardized Staff Leadership Program (SSLP) is a staff leadership/staff management, professional development, and school operations program (a component of SBC programming).

Three Ps: Production, Prosperity, and Promotional Growth
The three Ps define the scope of an individual's state of self-actualization: his ability to produce, prosper, and promote growth for self and for others.

Foreword

Mary E. Diez, Alverno College

This book could be seen as the story of a personal journey of a young African American teacher who grew up in the inner city; found her strengths as a learner, teacher, and administrator; and created a school that provided a rich learning environment for children facing the challenges of poverty.

This book is indeed the compelling story of that journey, but it would be a mistake to think that the story ends there. There are powerful lessons beyond the personal in these pages, lessons that can help all of us as educators rethink how we "do school"—and especially how we create learning environments of empowerment for children in our neediest inner-city communities.

Many school renewal or reform efforts purport to have "the answer" for how to rethink schooling, but most focus narrowly on only one area. No Child Left Behind erred, I believe, in making the assumption that more testing was the lynchpin for increasing achievement. Some narrow approaches to content standards miss the mark by focusing only on input, without recognizing the interaction between learners and content in its application in realistic contexts. Outside of the character education movement, not many approaches to reform recognize the role of the student as a person with a meaningful voice in the learning process. The effort to create the Preparatory School for Global Leadership (PSGL) addressed seven principles that should be integral to any school renewal or reform effort. All of these principles work together and reinforce the impact on learners that leads to their empowerment.

Living these principles, Ms. Dye and her teachers implemented a set of processes that provided support for the students on all levels of their learning. These courageous educators organized their school by providing students with basic knowledge on which to build, with opportunities to apply and deepen knowledge through both research projects and service learning, and with experiences and strategies to develop self-understanding and strength of character. The principles outlined in this book and the processes of living them out provide a solid road map to guide *how* to rethink schooling.

One key process was the yearly portfolio, which I experienced several times as I visited the school as a community volunteer. The portfolio was built on a set of explicit expectations about student learning and progress. The portfolio gave the students a sense of the larger picture of what school was about—in terms of their academic growth as well as their personal growth. In the portfolio process at the end of each year, students at PSGL documented and reviewed their work over the year, and presented their portfolio to a group including a teacher, a parent, a community member, and two or three peers. I remember sitting in on a set of these portfolio presentations in the first year of the school and being amazed at sixth graders talking about their evidence for demonstrating their "autonomy" in learning, one of the interpersonal assets that guided their movement toward empowerment. They were able to describe the change in their attitude and behavior as they worked on autonomy—for example, telling how they grew in their ability to get down to work in Project Block without their teacher or peers having to push them.

Another process was the daily interaction with adults about what was happening. I witnessed students participating in group meetings, where they raised issues and, in dialogue with their teacher, worked toward solutions. The impact of developing student voice and social interaction skills was evident at a community dinner held to celebrate the end of the school's second year. A young woman was called up to speak about her experience at the school and her remarks went something like this:

> In my old school, teachers always told me to sit down and shut up. If I wanted to argue against a teacher's decision, no one would listen and besides that I'd be in trouble for trying. But here, Ms. Dye and the teachers encourage us to raise issues and to make a good case for what we want to have happen. We don't always win, but we feel respected. They really listen.

Thus, empowerment was not just a term at PSGL; it lived in the skills of negotiation and argument nurtured in the students and in the openness of the staff to really listen to the students' perspectives.

Another process that is important to note as you read this book is the work required to build the adult community to support this kind of work. Teachers did not always come to PSGL with the kind of understanding of the aim of empowerment or the skills necessary to develop all aspects of the learners. Key aspects of their growth, like that of the students, included discussions of principles, practice with new approaches, and shared responsibility—with each other and with the students. Reform or renewal that leads to empowerment will call for this kind of work in any school that attempts it.

As you read this book, you will be struck by the complexity of the structure. Do not be put off by that, but probe how the seven principles are embedded in the structure and methods to support them. If you do, I promise that you will begin to think differently about what it will take to really fulfill the promise of education for learners, especially those in America's inner cities.

Milwaukee, Wisconsin
May 19, 2011

Prologue: The Mission to Empower

"She did what!"

That was my mother yelling in the kitchen, which was the next room over from my bedroom. She had just received a phone call, and her response let me know that my secret was out of the bag.

I should have known that this was the call that would determine the fate of my behind (meaning that I was about to get a spanking). I had a funny feeling when the telephone rang. Maybe I had been on edge waiting for this call, knowing that sooner or later someone would find out what I had done.

In my mind, I still thought I was right. I felt justified in my decision to mail those letters. But the words of warning given by my classmate Tracy right before I dropped the letters in the mailbox had started to haunt me.

"I don't think you should do that," she advised me. We were doing our daily walk to school that Monday morning. And normally, we talked about what fifth graders usually talked about in their morning walks to school. Yet, that day was different. We were not talking about how "fine" Brian was (the boy in our class whom all the girls were hot over). We were not talking about how Ms. Cohen was showing favoritism to her kids (because we thought that her role as a mother always overrode her role as our teacher when her royal children were in need). And we certainly were not talking about how our parents made us sick because there was something that weekend they would not let us do.

Instead, that morning was different . . . and the difference started with me. That bright Monday morning, I felt very inspired, charged, almost spiritually driven, because I felt like that day I was taking the first step that would change the world.

It was simply what I wanted to do. I wanted to change the world. I did not want to cause problems. I wanted to be in the position to make problems go away. I had gotten so sick and tired (and I can distinctly recall these feelings of frustration) of people complaining about how the world ought to be and doing absolutely nothing about it. And that morning, with the mailing of my letters, I was taking the first steps to be different and to also make a difference.

But my classmate said, "You can get into a lot of trouble."

I think in the back of my mind, I sort of knew this, but my vision of change was so strong, so compelling, that I allowed the mission of these letters to override any other sense of logic—of what my place as a little ten-year-old girl should be. I felt like I just had to mail them.

I had been hearing talk throughout my family about specific members within the family. I never questioned for a second if others loved the people under discussion the way I loved them. Deep down, I knew they were loved! I just felt that these individuals were acting in a way that was causing concern by the family at large. So, if these people I loved so dearly and only wanted the best for could correct their actions, we would achieve family harmony.

At my age, I did not understand that this act of venting out family frustration with other family members is almost a typical phenomenon within families. All I understood at the time was that these two individuals could grow and could become better people if only someone would take the time to tell them the error of their ways. So, that weekend, I pulled out some paper and I wrote two very purposeful letters. I told them all that I had heard and pleaded for them to make better choices. After writing these letters, which took me some time to convey both admonition and corrective direction, I proudly got two envelopes from my mother's personal desk and went to the corner store to purchase two stamps.

I was very proud of myself . . . of what I had committed to do. I believed in my actions and truly believed that it would be the start of a movement. And this is what I told Tracy.

"There is a lot of change needed in the world. Why not start with my family? Once I fix my family, I will then move on to fixing the world."

With that declaration and my self-proclaimed mission to be a social change agent, and Tracy slowly shaking her head, I dropped those letters into the mailbox.

Needless to say, the letters made it to their destination and the author of those letters was discovered. Even though I signed the letters "Anonymous," I still used words like "grandma" and "grandpa." Since I was the oldest grandchild (and by then people could justly attach this action to being my MO), they figured out that I did write those letters and quickly made a call to my mother letting her know what I had done.

My mother prepared to spank me that day. When she got off the phone, she told me to go get her belt. But then she started to laugh. I think she was bewildered that I would go through so much effort to do something so obviously ridiculous (as seen in the mind of an adult). So by the time she finished laughing, the anger had passed and something greater had set in—curiosity and the need to find the teachable moment in this situation.

I tried to tell her what I told Tracy. The world as I knew it needed to be fixed. And I felt that if I did not do anything about it, I was just as guilty as the people doing wrong.

I am not sure how that conversation ended, or how peace was made within the family (because it did cause some friction), but I think back on this situation often when I look at my life's work and choices I have made as a professional woman.

I want to see problems of the world fixed, and I believe that I, in some shape, form, or fashion, should be a part of the solution.

BEFORE I BECAME A CHANGE AGENT

Although my childhood desire of wanting to save the world stayed with me all the way through middle school and on into high school, it was actually in college that I began to understand the problems that needed to be fixed.

At age twenty, I enrolled in a social science degree program at a local all-women's college and began learning about social norms, group think, and economic distribution, along with studying the dynamic intricacies of social "isms" (classism, racism, sexism, etc.). From those studies, my deep desire to make a difference was validated and my childhood letter campaign was truly understood.

As a child, I saw disparity, oppression, and even violence. But I could also see prosperity, liberation, and peace. I sort of lived between two worlds. In my formative years, I lived with both of my parents, who exposed me to a lifestyle very different from the one they experienced in their impoverished youth.

Together, they accomplished the unbelievable task of building a home in a highly affluent community, miles away from the city; sending me to the neighborhood school (even if for only a short period); and therefore, exposing me to children and their families whose worlds represented that of the "privileged."

But by age eight, my parents had divorced, which then exposed me to a different life altogether—that of a single-parent household. It was through this experience that I spent a considerable amount of time in the inner city at my grandmother's house, where my aunts, uncles, grandparents, and the neighbors had the collective responsibility of watching my little sister and me.

And while I believe this experience exposed us to core values on love, community, and responsibility, this world also exposed me to societal oppression at its greatest.

Even though I could not articulate it, I was able to see the manifestation of powerlessness in many dimensions. Maybe not all in the same space and certainly not all within the immediate block where I played, but there was a pervasive sense of powerlessness in my world that was revealed through a lifestyle of poverty (and all that it entailed).

I think my mother still did a wonderful job as a single parent providing for us so we could get a private education and live in a neighborhood where these issues were not so loud (at least not most of the time).

And somewhere between the two jobs, taking us back and forth between school and Grandma's house, she was able to find time to put us in extracurricular activities. Through this, she exposed us to dance, music, and sports (all of which my friends in my grandmother's neighborhood did not have and all of which my friends in the suburbs had without question).

I am a very vigilant person, and I was vigilant even as a child. Although I did not know how to ask the questions, I wanted some answers to the social gaps I experienced. I saw the gaps as a universal problem, not just one that was experienced in my neighborhood, and for this, I wanted someone to come up with a universal solution.

Believing then, as I do now, that every person must take up a piece of the fight, as we each have a part of the solution to share, I had a burning desire to do my part to fix the problem. I wanted to make the world a better place.

I graduated from college in 1995 with a social science degree and a license to teach. While I eventually evolved to embrace the fundamental traits of effective teaching, my initial aim was never about the academics.

Instead, it was about social change. I wanted to be in a position to inspire people from my world so that in spite of their circumstances, they could rise up and live a life of production, prosperity, and promotional growth.

My goal over the past fifteen years has been about that steady focus to help disadvantaged individuals and communities live above the line. From my work as a teacher and a curriculum writer, to a community organizer, entrepreneur, and school administrator, my childhood desires to make a difference has been my driving force through it all.

The year in which I wrote this book was a time I took to stop, reflect, and regroup. In my relentless race to fix, I felt it was critical that I examine the journey and reevaluate the process. In doing so, I have been able to see the work on a whole new level. I have discovered some truths that could only come by way of living as a social change agent and then reflecting on it.

This book is about this experience, it is about some lessons that I have been able to uncover regarding the problem of social oppression, and it is about my personal revelations regarding the solution of education that I believe could truly make a difference.

I do not proclaim to be the end-all expert on issues relating to race and class. But with my degrees, certifications, and professional accomplishments with students, as well as my life experiences as an urban individual, I do proclaim to be an expert in urban education.

My professional experiences in urban education, along with my personal childhood struggles, qualify me to share. I think I have something to say that warrants consideration in the national discussion on social change, school reform, and the urban experience.

My work with empowerment serves as my version of a social solution. Through this book, I hope to have an impact on children I will never meet. With my words and your application, I believe we can empower the urban community.

MY JOURNEY INTO URBAN EDUCATION

There is a lot of irony in how I became a teacher. From my childhood, my college experiences, and my initial jobs as a political staff assistant and a community leader, no one would have thought that I would have ended up in the classroom.

In spite of it all, I am very thankful for my journey. In the process of finding me, I received my initial training for becoming a strong urban educator.

I am not sure if I was ever officially labeled as being an "at-risk" student; however, in retrospect, I certainly fit the bill. We never really did qualify for free or reduced lunch (one of today's indicators for being at risk). But in spite of my mother's ingenious ability to keep us one step above the poverty line, I did have a home that significantly disconnected me from the schooling experience.

There was physical and verbal abuse, and there was emotional turmoil and abandonment. From these experiences, I found myself also dealing with low self-esteem, shame, and guilt. And although my mother always found a way to pull through as "mama," there were times when I did not know if we were going to be OK.

It was a lot for me to carry on my own.

By the time I made it to high school, I had learned how to retreat inward to survive. When looking at what were giants to me in my home life, school was far smaller in comparison. So I withdrew.

While I knew academics were important for my future, I somehow could not muster up enough concern for my future. I was consumed with the pain that festered within (not really having a healthy outlet in which it could be addressed).

Instead of doing school, I focused on doing me (what I thought was me). I skipped school, and I stayed home and slept.

I skipped so much that I technically failed my junior year. While I never received a notice of failure, I did not earn any credits that year.

Having enough credits from my freshman and sophomore years to carry me through, I was able to enter my fourth year of high school as a senior.

It was not that I skipped school to party. Quite the contrary. I stayed home to hide out, to retreat, and to sleep. By my senior year, I had a boyfriend whom I had successfully pulled into my hiding place. And we skipped and hid together.

My friends did not understand how I skipped school just to stay at home. I will be honest. I tried several times to hang out with them during the day, but it was not as attractive as my bed. In my sleep, I did not have to face things that had no solutions.

Professionally, I understand now that I was depressed in high school. And I was also angry. So, like most teenagers who have unresolved depression and anger, I eventually found my way to some type of chemical substance that would allow me to escape it all.

Marijuana was scary to me because it was illegal. So I did not indulge in it even though my friends did. Yet as a forbidden fruit, alcohol did have an intriguing quality. I did not indulge often because although I was depressed, I still had a healthy fear of getting in trouble.

But I did go to school once under the influence. And even though it was only one time, I still think of that day with great sadness.

It was a day that I had to give a presentation in driver's education. I was petrified. I had been teased so much by my peers that the thought of getting in front of them to speak really frightened me. So, I strategized my support system.

There was no one I could go to to discuss my emotional deficits and fears. In my family, being emotional was considered weak. If I found the courage to speak up about my sadness or my fears, I was told to just "suck it up."

And on that day, I did what I needed to do so I could go into that classroom and "suck it up." I purchased the alcohol, took it to school, and consumed it about twenty minutes before the presentation. Sometimes I wonder why the teacher ignored what I had done. Surely he had to have known. But whether he did or not, I got away with it, getting a B+ on my presentation.

Not only did I have my share of experiences with truancy and teenage drinking, but I also had my share of fights. I did not fight because I was a bully. But I did fight to keep myself from being bullied.

Considering my low self-esteem, I was a prime target to be picked on in school. I truly believe that the only thing that stopped me from getting bullied was that I was good with physical self-defense.

It took only one time for people to physically threaten me in a new environment for them to learn that I would not be physically dominated. While I did not know how to defend myself verbally when I got teased in school, I could definitely defend myself physically when challenged.

And that is how I made it through high school, primarily skipping and sleeping through the confusion, with a couple of episodes of drinking and fighting. Through this method, I found a way to deal with the emotional chaos of my life.

I knew that my way of experiencing school was wrong. Although I owned my actions and my choices, I did not feel like the total blame rested on me. I felt that my problems were a part of a bigger issue.

I do not think I was sophisticated enough in my thoughts then to blame specific individuals or institutions for my challenges with school. However, I knew on some gut level that my struggles were social more than they were academic.

I think it was this interest I had in social change that motivated me enough to do the work to finally get into college. Although I eventually found myself promoting school and academics as a teacher, I entered college with my sights set only on social change.

When I enrolled in school, I took up social science as my major. There, I studied Richard Daft's theories on power and dependency. I examined Karl Marx's views on the haves and have-nots. And I worked hard to incorporate the "life, liberty, and the pursuit of happiness" principles of John Locke, Thomas Jefferson, and Sir William Blackstone into my study on social solutions.

I did not yet know how I was personally going to be a part of a solution, but I did find great fulfillment in learning the problem and considering the possibilities.

So how did I get into education?

Well, the school I went to had a programming requirement for its students. You were to choose a major, and also carry two supports (or two minors). If, however, you added education to your study, you did not have to pick up another support. They would allow education to singularly fulfill the two-minor condition.

Therefore, I did not choose education as part of my career plan. I chose it simply because it was a way for me to bypass the two-minor requirement.

I wish I could say something a little more profound about how I found my way into the classroom, but it is true. I got a teaching license because I thought it was a faster way to get through school.

But that clearly was not the case.

Being an education student, you were required to complete four semesters of field study and one semester of student teaching. As a field student, you went into the class to support another teacher. By helping to set up the room, helping to correct papers, and helping to provide students with one-on-one support, you got a feel of the teaching profession and you got a chance to personally explore some of the teaching frameworks you were studying in class.

Then as a student teacher, you got a chance to see how you personally fit into the mode of full-time teaching, and you learned who you were as a practitioner. While under the supervision of a primary teacher, you developed your own lessons, personally led in instruction, and single-handedly directed the day-to-day demands of classroom management.

And that is what I did.

I completed course work required for the education degree while simultaneously fulfilling the requirements for the social science degree (constituting a double major), along with the four semesters of field studies and the one semester for student teaching. All the work I did in the classroom, I did without compensation, so I also had to go out and work in order to pay for utilities, groceries, and so on.

In hindsight, choosing education was good for me (as this is what I was destined to do); yet it certainly was not the easy route.

I have yet to talk about my experiences as a student teacher and field student. However, it is important for me to acknowledge that my approach with student empowerment actually started in those classrooms.

Somehow without fully knowing why, I was able to create lessons that engaged students, and I was able to inspire them to want to meet my classroom expectations for behavior. Ultimately (which is to me the most significant part of my work as a teacher in training), I was able to present education to my students as their ticket to improve their lives.

I can clearly see that the instructional framework that I now cherish as being the model for urban empowerment was right there from the beginning. I did not know how I was doing what I was doing, but I definitely was doing it.

With such a natural connection to teaching and students, along with the consistent praise that I received from my instructors and supervisors, one would think that I would have considered a career in education. Although I did not choose teaching as a profession when I entered college, it could be argued that teaching had clearly chosen me.

But I did not see it. I was still focused on social change, and I was not mature enough to see the connection it had with education.

My run from the classroom was not really about my own experiences as a student. By this time, I could see how my struggles in high school helped me relate effectively to my students.

And of course, as with some of my classmates who went into teaching and quickly left, it was never because I could not deal with the dynamics of urban education.

Honestly, I was drawn to those dynamics. I had to have been, as I had developed a pattern of working in those environments even when it was not required.

Regardless of my schedule, I found a way to volunteer as a Girl Scout leader and as a volleyball coach. And I personally took up the mantle of formally mentoring my younger cousins and their friends.

Even before going to college, in my transitional year after high school when I vowed that I would never set foot into another school building, I actually started a pompom squad for inner-city teenage girls. This was not a paid job. It was not even an agency-supported program. I did all the work to locate resources for practice, for uniforms, and for transportation just so I could be a role model to a group of disadvantaged yet extremely impressionable and loving young girls.

I loved the connection that I had with urban children. Heck, I was urban. I had a knack for teaching even when I had not formally been assigned to teach. And deep down I knew that these young people needed me to see them and their needs, just as I had needed someone to see me and mine when I was their age.

So I was not afraid to teach, to get tangled up with the some of the ugly challenges in urban education, and I certainly was not afraid of the feisty energy that is given off by the average teenager (which is often misunderstood as attitude or disrespect).

I think I just could not see teaching as a viable way to fulfill my life's mission for social change.

Besides, there were more teachers in my world who were disgruntled with the system of education than those who were inspired. I felt that my colleagues (not all, but enough to scare me) were angry about their work, disconnected from the real reasons why they went into teaching, and jaded about their lack of power to make a difference.

I did not want that to be me. I wanted to feel like I could make a difference, and I wanted to be happy doing it. So while embracing my studies in education as a student, I did not want to embrace them as a professional.

Well, I *tried* not to.

First, I took an internship with the U.S. Department of Education in Washington, D.C., where I worked with the federal government on a number of national projects. I worked to facilitate a national satellite town hall meeting; I worked to publish a national school directory for private schools; and I attended congressional hearings on the Hill, updating my department on issues relating to education.

Once the internship was completed, I returned to Wisconsin and negotiated a position with the City of Milwaukee. It was believed at the time that my degrees in social science and secondary education would be a great fit for work in community programming.

There, I helped high school dropouts get leadership and entrepreneurial training while they were picking up a technical trade and studying for their GED. As the program's coordinator, I was responsible for establishing the administrative umbrella for the whole program, as well as developing the curriculum (and instructional staff) for the leadership and entrepreneurial course work.

But while I knew I was making a difference, I did not believe I was making the difference I had made when I was a student teacher.

After six months on the job, I prayed. I thanked God for the work I currently had because it was a job that was basically created just for me.

But I wanted to have more clarity on my purpose for social change, and I wanted to make sure that I was doing what I was supposed to do, as opposed to doing what I wanted to do.

I believed that doing what I was supposed to do would give me the fulfillment that I did not feel in my current position.

So as I prayed for fulfillment, I also vowed that I would perform to the best of my ability in my current job until a better fit came along. I refused to allow myself to send out résumés, and I refused to allow myself to make phone calls to people I thought could help me find a different job.

I think I was somehow testing destiny. If it was meant for me to work somewhere else, the job would come to me. I would not have to go to it.

It was Thursday when I prayed. On Friday, I received a call from someone who worked in the mayor's office. One of her principal-friends had called in a bind, looking for a good teacher who could effectively teach disadvantaged youth middle school social studies and language arts.

She knew I had the talents and the social studies license, and she felt obligated to let me know about the position. That fall, I started my first full-time teaching position, at an urban Catholic school.

It was in this experience that I understood my work with urban education. In the classroom, I was able to unleash my talents on student empowerment. Through this realization, my specific assignment for social change became clear.

By empowering students, I was equipping them to face their future, to use education to protect themselves and their family, and to own the reality that if any achievement and change was ever going to happen in their lives, it was going to come by way of their efforts. Because only they could break the cycle of poverty, pain, and powerlessness they may have been experiencing.

My approach with empowerment gave students the power that they needed to be more than victims, to be more than recipients, to be more than powerless.

And for this reason, I found an immense amount of fulfillment in teaching. I was able to make a difference. I had found my place in social change.

MY WORK AS A TEACHER

For the next ten years of my life, I spent my time growing as a classroom teacher. I learned the needs of my students, relating to them as much as possible, yet finding and embracing their differences.

And I learned how to sharpen my craft with empowerment via curriculum development, instruction, and student management—because I never, not even for one second, forgot why I was assigned to my work as a teacher. I was there to be a social change agent.

It was a funny thing, my disposition as a classroom teacher. While I believed I was good at what I did and I was good because it was what I was destined to do, it was very exhausting. My hours were ridiculously long, as the demands of the classroom seemed to be never-ending.

Taking the standard job description for teaching and then coupling it with the mission for urban empowerment, there were periods where I ceased to function as Angela the person and consumed myself with being Ms. Dye the change agent.

I remember my father coming over to my house because he was worried about me. He said, "You work a job to live, not live to work a job." And honestly, that was what I was doing.

It took some years for me to figure out how to have balance between work and home. I eventually did learn the lesson.

Ultimately, I think I had to learn how to wrestle with the mission. Teaching was simply not just a job for me. I believed it was a spiritual calling. And, therefore, I was personally invested.

You see, I was frequently reminded of the real issues facing our students outside of the school. I understood what life for them was like when they went home. Because when I went home, I continued to see my students (and the issues they faced).

For example, there was the story of Chris, the son of my aunt's friend. When I went home, I would see him at age thirteen standing on the corner. I knew Chris had not been in school all day, and I knew he was not standing on the corner just to wave at traffic. He was there making a living—illegally.

I felt heavy because I wondered how the education system had failed him.

I would get out of my car, talk to Chris about school, about life, about choices. I tried to become his teacher in increments of time.

I once did some work in the school where he was a third grader, and I was able to talk with his classroom teacher. I knew he was significantly behind in his academics. And while he was promoted from grade level to grade level, Chris never learned the basics. Therefore, he never caught up—he was always behind his classmates.

So, by the time he made it to eighth grade, it was easier for him to just give up. He left that environment where he was failing and redefined success in a way that was suitable for him.

The story of Chris is not unusual for teachers who teach in low-income communities. But the story of Chris was more than just usual for me. As a neighbor and a friend, to come home and see daily reminders of how schooling was not the solution, I could not just leave the issues when I left work. I only faced them again when I got home.

I had to face friends who had turned to prostitution, drugs, and welfare, and I had to face myself—because I too, being from this community, had my own personal issues to continually contend with.

So with these very real, in-your-face reminders of what education should be and what it had failed to be for a specific community of people, I worked. And I worked. And I worked.

I had to persistently find ways to instructionally empower my students to tackle their personal and social demons.

And, trust me, my classroom was not based on sitting around discussing and crying over our personal problems.

Not by a long shot.

My instruction was standards based, research driven, and academically sound. It was my aim to kill two birds with one stone. I taught the academics of social studies, language arts, and even reading in order to teach students how to change their circumstances.

Through it all, I learned that there was an emotional state that was pervasive among students. It was not only that students were contending with the realities of urban living, but there was also a sense of powerlessness that they had inherited and, indirectly, championed.

Students acted in ways that were destructive because they operated within a personal construct that was destructive.

Even students who were considered to be "good students" did not have a full sense of who they were and what they had the potential to do. I wrestled with these students (and their parents the most), because they had somehow been judged and graded based on the failure of their peers. Because they were performing one or two steps ahead, they had been tricked into believing that they were high achievers.

But their performance was relative, and when they were put in a different environment, their "A" track record would not be enough to navigate through a world where achievement required more.

This limited space of achievement had happened to one of my aunts. She received a scholarship to attend Marquette University because of her 4.0 grade point average at a neighborhood school in the inner city. Yet after she got there, she struggled. She really had not been prepared for their learning climate. While her scores were high, she did not have the skills or the emotional strength to do the politics associated with how the new environment defined achievement.

So my work involved pushing my students toward personal power and strength. And to give shape to a universal framework of achievement, I used state-based standards.

I never used the bell curve (which simply determines the number of students who can receive an A and the number of students who are expected to receive an F). I did not set my students up to compete with each other like this.

I wanted them to be able to compete with life.

Therefore, I dangled before them a picture of achievement, and then I got in the trenches to help them find their own power to achieve.

Another way I created a universal framework for achievement was by using rubrics. I became the queen of rubrics. Through a rubric, a teacher (and even a parent) can clearly paint a picture of achievement. It does not allow achievement to exist as some mythical entity only to be interpreted with subjectivity after the performance has been rendered.

Transforming my students from a place of powerlessness to a place of power did present me as a witch. And when graced with that name by my students (replacing the *w* with a *b*), I thanked my students. Because I knew then I was doing my job.

Change does not come without discomfort. That name meant that I was making them uncomfortable. And, ultimately for me, it meant that I was not buying into the institution of their destruction.

I loved my students, so being mean was not my objective. But I was not just there to teach—I was there to empower. So in doing so, I held them accountable to a standard of achievement. I held them accountable to a mission.

Somewhere in the beginning of the second semester (if it was my first year with the students), a transformation would occur. Students realized that I was not "playing school." They saw my discipline differently. It became less and less personal. Over time, students began to understand that in my classroom, accountability was not about malice, it was about mission.

Not only did students learn from me, but as I really studied them and worked on my discipline, I learned from them.

I learned that students do not want to be told that they have a future. They need to see that they have a future (one that realistically embraces who they are).

Students do not need to know that knowledge is power. They want to know that power is already within them and that it is OK to use that power.

Students do not need to learn about reading/writing/math as a virtue. They need to learn about it as a form of survival.

Students do not need to learn about the past or about the world because it is good for them to know. They need to learn about the past and about the world because it will help them deal with their present circumstances.

Students should not be expected to do the right things. They should be expected to define what is right and should be allowed to barter and negotiate when what they want differs from what we want for them.

Students should not be told (directly or indirectly, explicitly or implicitly) who they are and then trained to be something that someone else wants them to be. They need to authentically see for themselves who they are and then be given the opportunity and the training to become the person they want to be.

Students do not need to be stripped of their power when they are being held accountable for their actions. They need to use their power in order to participate in the accountability process, allowing them to authentically learn and grow from the experience.

These points have stayed with me in my career as an educator. First, I learned to structure my classroom, my projects, and my instruction based on these lessons. And eventually, once I formalized my philosophy of empowerment and my instructional method for empowerment, I found a way to create learning principles that embraced the education that they have given me.

The more I became aware of the psychosocial dimension to teaching and learning, the more effective I became as a teacher. I grew to understand the scientific value of my pedagogy, which truly was with me from day one (in my days as a student teacher).

Through it all, I learned how to strategically and methodically transform the destructive and helpless nature of my learners.

I learned how to empower them with intention.

FORMATION OF A CURRICULUM AND A SCHOOL

As I taught and perfected my craft, I learned more and more how to empower with intention. At the same time, I found myself evolving into an instructional leader.

I was asked to take on a roster of the more difficult students. I was called on to train other teachers. And I was invited to develop high school courses. I had even begun to compile my signature projects into an instructional model that I loosely named Social Being and Change (SBC).

By this time, I had begun to publicly articulate my mission for social change and state my intentions of empowerment as an educator. I was not exactly sure as to the specifics, but I knew there was more for me to do with my work. So I went back to school and pursued a master's of education in administration and instructional leadership.

Although I came out with two leadership licenses (one to run a school and the other to direct the development of curriculum), I could not really see myself in those traditional roles. I know now that it was not that I resisted leadership, I just wrestled with the platform in which I was to lead.

I love the authentic feel of grassroots initiatives. This is what I did in college when I organized the community pom-pom squad. And it was what I did in fifth grade, when I launched my letter-writing campaign to save the world.

I enjoy being in situations where I can make a direct impact with the people I am serving. And my perception of school leadership was that I would not be able to directly connect with my students. As a result, I prematurely concluded that as a school administrator, I would not be able to empower them.

But it is an interesting thing how the universe works when you get connected to your life's purpose. Regardless of my perceptions, my background, my politics, or my resources, destiny would have its way.

Now as I speak with this faith, it is important to admit that my faith has not always been as such. Truthfully, it has been an evolution, as I have watched my purpose be proven over and over again. I do not talk about it much in this book, but there were many times that I tried to deny that education was the way to fulfill the mission of social change.

But because I believe in the concept of divine assignment, I submit to a level of unselfishness. I pray for a clear vision and the right spirit to both accept and do the work that I am required to do.

There were three "experiences" that got me to embrace my work with launching the curriculum as a school, even though deep down inside of me, I was just a little girl with the mission to only mail letters.

The first experience was the encouragement of my friends and colleagues. As a teacher, they saw something in my classroom that they believed could be turned into a school. Not knowing anyone else was speaking these words to me, they both found ways to challenge me with the idea of pursuing a charter school contract.

It was the second experience that led me to begin to take the idea of starting a school seriously. It was a paper I had written when I returned to pursue my graduate degree. I was required to write about an ideal school. Through that paper, I discussed my ideas on a schoolwide approach to student empowerment (through the full alignment of my SBC curriculum with programming, policies, and operations).

I happened to have the dean of the graduate program as my instructor. And while her presence was nerve wracking to most of us in the class (because, like me, she was a no-nonsense, no-excuses, high-standards kind of teacher), the feedback she gave me on that assignment spoke to me on a spiritual level.

In blue ink sprawled across my paper, she wrote something that went like this, "Very inspiring, Angela. You should think about starting this."

Of course, I questioned in my mind why in the world she would think that I could actually start a school. But in my spirit, I knew that the universe was using someone I immensely respected to echo a message I had been ignoring.

So five years after I graduated from college (undergrad) and eleven years after I crawled my way out of high school, I accepted that I was to take my classroom mission of empowerment to the schoolwide level.

But acceptance and execution are two separate things.

It was not until this third experience with one of my students that I finally moved forward to do the work.

By this time, I was teaching in another state. And although there was a difference in the cultural climate, I found that the need for empowerment was still present.

I will say, however, these students took empowerment to another level. Through them, I was able to see the vision of empowerment, and I got a better understanding of the power of my work.

Yet even though I saw a new level of empowerment, I still operated under fear. Teaching had become safe for me. I had finally learned to work with balance, meaning that I no longer had to put in ridiculous hours to get the desired results in my classroom. And I knew I would lose that balance if I did in fact step out to launch the school.

So while my classroom became a place of empowerment for my students, it also served as a hiding place for me, as I ran from my charter school assignment. Because it was easier for me to do something I was good at than to do something I had never experienced, I fooled myself into believing that this new level of empowerment (in that classroom and in that school) was the ultimate work that I was destined to do.

It was William, my sixth-grade student, who challenged the illusion I had started to create.

While I do not remember the lesson I was teaching that day, I do remember William struggling with his hands. He put them up. And then, he put them down. He put them up again. And then again, he put them down.

I knew he wanted something, and I also knew that it was something that he was not quite comfortable asking. So after watching him struggle a bit about his decision to ask me or to not ask me, I finally questioned him, "What is it, William? Do you have something to say?"

His response was, "I do, but I do not want to get in trouble."

Because I strongly believe in student voice (which is a part of my philosophy of empowerment, which I will later go on to explain), I said, "You can speak freely and I promise that you will not get in trouble. Just make sure that you keep your tone respectful."

I remember the students watching this interplay between William and me. At this point in the school year, they knew that I encouraged students to speak freely. Therefore, they knew William was not going to get in trouble if he did say something offensive. But they still were curious as to what he wanted to ask me.

And, this is what he said:

"Ms. Dye, you are always talking to us about empowerment—about being leaders and not followers, being employers not employees." He went on to say, "Why are you teaching? Aren't you working for someone? When are you going to start your own school?"

Of course there was a lot that I wanted to say to this young man. He was basically calling me a hypocrite (saying there was a gap between what I talked about and what I did).

And oh, I remember feeling challenged. I wanted to argue with him that there is nothing wrong with teaching. I wanted to defend that being a good teacher was my personal story of empowerment.

Heck! He did not know my history!

But honestly, it was not about what he knew. It was about what *I* knew. And I knew that this young man was being used to make me go beyond accepting my assignment. It was time for me to walk in it.

So when I went home that day, I started the work of launching the school.

And just in case I would be tempted to go back into hiding, God stripped me of my cave.

He took away my ability to teach in that state. For almost two years, I had used my teaching certification from Wisconsin. However, shortly after my conversation with William, I received a notice that my Wisconsin license would not be allowed for the following school year.

There was no choice for me but to leave. While I loved my new home, I knew I had to be where my teaching credentials were accepted.

So that summer, I moved back to Wisconsin.

The funny thing is that after I returned home, I did receive a teaching certification from the state I had left. I smiled when I opened the mail. To me, it was a confirmation that I did not leave the state because of my credentials. I left the state because of my assignment.

So for a year, I buckled down. I stepped outside of my comfort zone of being a teacher, and I became a politician, a community organizer, and a business manager. I created my start-up team, pursued my charter school contract, raised money, and recruited students and families to enroll in my school.

It was my own empowerment that moved me beyond a place of fear and powerlessness and into a place of purpose.

In 2004, I started Preparatory School for Global Leadership (PSGL), a small charter school authorized by Milwaukee Public Schools.

For five years, I served as the school's director and principal, working hard to use SBC as a schoolwide model to empower urban learners.

IN CLOSING . . .

Sometimes I cringe when I think about how close I came to the other side, the side where your motivation in life can be lost forever.

While my fifth-grade letter-writing campaign launched me as a social change agent, the challenges of my childhood eventually suffocated my vision, blinding me of my potential.

I have said several times throughout this chapter that my work with education has always been about social change, alluding to the fact that it was my plight to save my students. But in all honesty, I believe it was the plight of my students that actually saved me.

They gave me context. They gave me relevance. And they gave me purpose.

Now, as I take a moment to reflect on it all, I realize that empowerment really did start here.

Using the strong work ethic of my family, the tenacious strength of my mother, and the unconditional love of my students, I was able to bypass what so many others fall victim to.

This is the reason why I taught, why I started a school with only the skills of being a good teacher and all the passion of saving the world, and it is the reason why I am writing this book. There are so many students who are close to being lost forever. Sitting with all the power they need to make a difference for themselves, they do not know how to access it, activate it, and use it for their own good.

Empowerment is about the power that urban students need to transform their own lives. Unfortunately, our students do not have this power.

By reading about SBC and PSGL, my hope is that you will learn how to empower or they will learn how to empower themselves.

Future generations are depending on what they have hidden and locked inside.

ONE

The Construct of Empowerment

Preparatory School for Global Leadership (PSGL) gave me a different perspective of the Social Being and Change (SBC) model for empowerment. My work with empowerment as a classroom teacher required me to labor. However, my work with empowerment at PSGL required me to push.

Going into my role as the school's founding director, I thought the bulk of my job would be centered on the organization's development, instruction, and administration. Instead, there was a pocket of work that was there waiting for me that really caught me off guard.

I have always worked with disadvantaged students. Therefore, no one could have told me that I would wrestle with urban dynamics. Living the life and then having considerable experience teaching within it, I thought I knew, hands down, how to implement empowerment in any urban environment I would face.

In the past, the greatest challenge of empowerment centered on exposing the misconception of achievement. In these settings, I had to challenge students' perception of success. Somehow, they believed that their limited level of performance was acceptable and that it would be instrumental in having a successful life.

While others may not know how to get students to look at the limitations of their performance in a real and meaningful way, I was able to do this. And I did it as a natural part of my practice as a classroom teacher.

But my students at PSGL did not just struggle with their perception of achievement. They struggled with their perception of living.

I believed my students at PSGL came from a generational experience of powerlessness where the lifestyle is based on an institutionalized way of thinking. When a behavior or a thought becomes institutionalized, it

1

cannot be addressed simply by way of reading, writing, math, and standardized tests.

Instead, there has to be an instructional process that understands and embraces the psychological conditions of what it means to be a racial minority, to be poor, *and* to be academically challenged.

It took me some time to fully understand this psychological dilemma that I was faced with at PSGL, and as a result, it took me some time to modify the empowerment model to effectively wrestle with institutionalized patterns of poverty and oppression.

As the author of the curriculum, I became more sophisticated with my approach to empowerment. I made sure that the methodologies for empowerment were just as ruthless as my students' habits were for failure.

I did not have to change the intention of empowerment or its principles, but I did have to delve more into the methods.

Empowerment was no longer an opportunity. It was a mandate. It became our institutionalized approach for achievement to combat an institutionalized approach for destruction.

In this chapter, I want to take a look at the principles of empowerment as a philosophy. While they are the basis of the SBC curriculum, they really can exist as a stand-alone presence in any school, classroom, home, or community organization.

If you are working with a population of people who seem to express a pervasive sense of powerlessness by way of their thoughts, their behaviors, or their decisions, you can use these principles to create policies that will put power in places where there is none.

If you are reading this book, I am sure you are interested in *how* we employed the principles of empowerment as methods. You are not just interested in theoretical frameworks. So, rest assured, sharing with you concrete methods of empowerment is what I intend to do.

In chapters 2 to 7, I will discuss five specific programs that we used at PSGL to combat dispositions of failure.

But in this chapter, I want to equip you with the philosophy and principles of empowerment to give you a better understanding of why we did what we did at PSGL, as well as how we did it.

I also want to empower you to generate your own approach to the empowerment principles so that you can meet the unique needs of your own environment.

Whether you are an administrator, a teacher, a parent, or a community leader, I share this framework so you can join me in the mission for social change.

LEARNED HELPLESSNESS

Have you ever looked at someone from a distance and questioned why they made the choices they were making? From your angle, you can clearly see a cause-and-effect relationship where there is a strong correlation between behavior and negative outcomes.

This is especially true if you are a parent dealing with a fussy toddler. If only the baby had gone to sleep as you had planned, he would not be so tired and cranky.

Not only do we see things from a different perspective when we are parents, but we also see them from different perspectives when we are colleagues, friends, and lovers. If only you had reported to work on time, you would not have gotten fired. If only you had told the truth, you would not have gotten into trouble. If only you had studied, you would not have failed the test.

Based on our level of wisdom, life experience, insight, or maturity, we are able to predict negative outcomes to poor choices.

But when you are in a leadership position, it is not enough to look at the cause-and-effect relationship of someone's choices. We need to understand why that person makes the choices that to us are so clearly destructive. Once we understand why, then we can create systems that will deal with the motivating factor within the choice, not just simply redirect the person from making them.

Learned helplessness looks at the motivation to why students fail. It does not take a rocket scientist for someone to figure out that a student failed a test because he did not study. But it takes someone with a little more skill and training to look at why a student failed to study even though he or she knew it was required to pass the test.

As this is not a theory that initially was created to look at student behavior, it is not a theory that has to be limited to student behavior.

If you are reading this book and you are not a teacher or a parent, it still may benefit you to examine the theory. Because through this theory, you will be able to understand your own choices that have led to negative outcomes in your life and, as a result, to zero in on a solution that addresses the problem at the root level of behavior (where it exist).

Of course, a lot of material has been produced covering the concept of learned helplessness, but in my attempt to write to the layperson and empower the unempowered, I will try to simplify the theory so that it can be embraced by an audience not typically engaged in academic research.

In short, the theory states that our behavior that causes pain is not made by a conscious choice for pain but by a subconscious choice for comfort.

Starting with the exploration of animal behavior, scientists discovered that repeated associations between discomfort and a specific behavior caused the behavior to persist even when the discomfort was no longer associated with the experience.

When the subject is ineffective in stopping the discomfort, he resorts to a place of acceptance where he embraces the discomfort as a way of being. Even when the discomfort is removed, the subject, becoming so accustomed to the discomfort, may act in ways to perpetuate the discomfort, as it becomes more uncomfortable to survive in its absence.

In the theory of learned helplessness, individuals fail, or engage in destructive behavior, not because they aspire for destruction but because destructive behavior somehow has some level of familiar comfort. To exist outside of this destruction would cause more discomfort than the actual destruction in itself.

Without going too deeply into matters of slavery, discrimination, and institutionalized racism (along with other social isms that could easily be applied), this historical presence of a subpar existence due to events beyond one's control can cause a community of people to set up a structure that embraces and perpetuates conditions of oppression.

When learned helplessness transfers from being an individual issue to a cultural phenomenon, not only can we see the existence of thought patterns and behaviors that are indicative of helplessness, but we also see the establishment of norms, institutions, and spiritual beliefs that serve as social reinforcement to this way of thinking.

By the time we make it into the schoolhouse, where we have the offspring of this mind-set—children of the oppressed and children of the oppressor—we have created an unintentional yet very distinctive space of institutionalized oppression.

At some point or another, we all have been children of both the oppressed and the oppressor, even when we try in earnest to fight against the lingering residue of our past. As a result, we reproduce what we know and inadvertently create systems and processes that promote comfort, failing to truly rattle the status quo in fear of causing discomfort; yet, ultimately, we create an instructional methodology that perpetuates the lifestyle of the oppressed.

Every curriculum that has ever been introduced into a classroom is shaped by some type of theoretical framework. And when we look at the curriculum and the learning modalities functioning within the inner-city experience, we cannot deny that the grounding philosophy centers on the unfortunate notion of tradition, a tradition that has been based on substandard living.

I want to detour a little bit to discuss Bloom's taxonomy, an educational framework by Benjamin Bloom. In it he states that there are varying levels of cognition. In order to reach the highest skill levels of synthesis and evaluation, one must know how to function at the lower levels of rote memorization, comprehension, and recall.

If applied correctly, this theory would get us closer to the place of combating learned helplessness. Students would be able to have the basic skills to function successfully on standardized tests and have the mental capacity to think critically about the world and find ways to successfully live within it.

Unfortunately, Bloom's taxonomy is rarely applied effectively in urban classrooms. Typically, one end of the spectrum or the other is emphasized, resulting in students experiencing frustration (not having the basic *skills* to engage in constructivist, high-end learning) or boredom (not having the *opportunity* to engage in constructivist, high-end learning).

As an urban educator, I understand how difficult it is to teach to the full range of cognition in classrooms where the learning levels are extremely varied. What do you do when you have eighth graders functioning at both the second-grade level and the twelfth-grade level, especially when you are bound to conventional systems such as fifty-minute class periods, standardized tests, and grade-level standards?

These restrictions, systemic grade-level deficiencies and variations, along with issues such as apathy, oppositional conflict, attention deficits, and depression can and do create a recipe for disaster.

Bloom's taxonomy, when it is correctly applied, can only speak to instruction. This is what traditional education has emphasized: instruction and the acquisition of knowledge and skills. But it also, in the context of social stratification, institutionalized inequities, and socioeconomic challenges, reinforces what already is. Instruction that emphasizes cognition, at its best, can only promote the status quo. It does not give students insight or the power to acquire the comfort they are ultimately seeking.

When students are bored and when they are frustrated, they will behave in ways, although destructive, that are only intended to provide a space for comfort.

The best way to maximize Bloom's taxonomy is to employ it in a system where students are powerful instead of powerless. We must allow the framework of Bloom's taxonomy and other scientifically proven strategies to create spaces of comfort for students. Continuing to force students to function in spaces of discomfort accelerates a need for them to create spaces of comfort. As a result, behaviors emerge that inadvertently work against long-term production, prosperity, and promotional growth.

Fortunately, or unfortunately, I have lived both experiences.

Coming from a background of a single parent, domestic violence, and alcoholic grandparents (my paternal and maternal grandfathers), one can clearly question the lifestyle choices of my world. And although I have grown to embrace formal education, and I work very hard to embrace my own principles of empowerment, I have to continually, on a daily basis, restructure my thinking that drives my natural inclination to seek short-term solutions for comfort.

From my training, and I believe from my spiritual liberation, I question my perception of comfort and try to discipline my behaviors to be driven toward self-actualization.

And even being an educator and now an author of empowerment, I cannot say this rethinking process is easy. I know that I have been guided under the premise of learned helplessness and that my journey toward production, prosperity, and promotional growth requires twice the work of my peers who do not have a lineage of oppression.

While I was fortunate to have my maternal grandmother, who forced my mother and her six siblings to embrace school as an opportunity, there were other forces that weighed me down and interfered with me fully seizing the opportunity of opportunity.

And basically, this is my point.

Even though we are living in an age of universal and equitable standards, we have not deinstitutionalized oppression. We have not transformed the mind-set of the community in which we are trying to serve. We have not emotionally positioned our students to seize the opportunity of opportunity.

You cannot liberate a group of people who have been oppressed economically, politically, and spiritually, who have established a framework of being that accepts the imposed boundaries of years ago, simply by giving them an opportunity.

People will only embrace an opportunity when they have been conditioned to see opportunity as an opportunity, not just by creed but by deed—by repeatedly seeing the living benefits of that opportunity. They must be given tools to see, to embrace, and to eventually apply.

This is what the empowerment model does by way of the seven principles of empowerment. It deals with the psychosocial aspect of the learner, connecting his world to the world of mainstream living, and positioning him to embrace the opportunity of opportunity.

While we have a dire need to promote all levels of cognition, we have to understand that the fundamental challenge of learning and self-actualizing does not rest solely in the mind. The problem that we must contend with is found within the spirit.

For this reason, empowerment is for the psyche as reading/writing/math is for the mind. It transforms the thinking of the powerless by giving them the psychological tools to be powerful.

EMPOWERMENT: THE ANTITHESIS

I would definitely agree that dealing with the existence of learned helplessness is quite a conundrum within the world of education. Regardless as to the whys of low performance of specific students, we are not able to limit our instruction to this experience.

To do so would only perpetuate the problem.

But ignoring the reality that students suffering from learned helplessness have different learning needs is not the answer either.

Students who come from oppressed backgrounds are not going to embrace formal education the way we desire—no matter the clarity and the complexity in which we develop academic standards, no matter the sanctions we levy on principals and school districts, and no matter the cultural training that we impose on teachers. Students who live a life of embedded failure will not be able to perform at high levels until there is a change in their perspective on being and achieving.

The empowerment model is based on a philosophy of self-actualization and the personal power needed to get there.

When we self-actualize, we become our best self by reaching our highest place of being in the physical sense of human living. It is about getting to a place where we are able to produce, to prosper, and to promote growth in ourselves and in others.

The concept of production, prosperity, and promotional growth is not dependent on what we know. And even though I am a champion of performance-based learning models, it is not even dependent on what we can do.

The concept of the three Ps, as I often refer to the production, prosperity, and promotional growth of self-actualization, is about how we streamline our perspective to those outcomes and how we position ourselves to achieve them.

It is about our power (which is also a right and a responsibility) to know, to do, and to be.

The empowerment philosophy draws upon seven distinct principles of defining, accessing, and applying the power that we need for the three Ps.

From principle one, which deals with P^3 Commitment (the mind-set to self-actualize) to principle seven, which deals with Shared Accountability (accountability measures that protect the self-actualization process), these principles constitute a thought pattern that takes one from existing as powerless to existing as powerful.

Through this psychosocial transformation, individuals are better prepared to produce, prosper, and promote growth.

INSTRUCTIONAL FRAMEWORK TO EMPOWERMENT

The empowerment framework does not have to be limited to the classroom. It can be applied to how we manage children at home. And it can be applied to a self-help model for adults, who know that they too suffer from learned helplessness. Through it, they can do the personal work of the seven principles in order to become more proactive, more powerful, in their own self-actualization.

But because my life's work of social change has been clearly channeled into instructional empowerment for adolescent learners, I thought it only fitting to dedicate my first book to the strategies of student empowerment.

It is important to note that empowerment as an instructional tool is the work we do as educators to teach students how to generate and use power for the sake of production, prosperity, and the promotion of growth in self and in others. For an empowerment-based environment, it is why we teach.

With this frame of reference, empowerment is *the instructional approach to teaching students how to self-assign power to achieve a life of production, prosperity, and promotional growth*.

Now, in order to teach under the principles of empowerment, students must first understand the concept of production, prosperity, and promotional growth before they can aspire to attain them.

The definitions of these three terms are fairly simple.

Production is the producing of outcomes by way of using skills, talents, and resources. Prosperity is a state of being that relates to success (however one defines success). And promotional growth is the ability to inspire personal growth in self and in others.

This personal growth relates to the intangible part of our being. It is about reaching the highest place of internal strength where our sense of self is aligned with our intentions and with our unique purpose on this earth.

When you teach to these three outcomes, you create vision in your classroom, in your school, in your household. You establish direction and focus, and you provide purpose for all of your endeavors.

This need for understanding the three Ps is foremost in the empowerment framework, because it sets the purpose for teaching and learning. It provides a vision of a tomorrow that separates students from the realities of their today. It gives students and teachers a daily mission, and it provides a necessary context for the learning environment.

The empowerment model as a whole deals with a culture of learning and development in the classroom. It is a way of teaching that fosters the self-actualization of our students.

Every classroom and every school has a culture, whether it is positive or negative, intentional or unintentional. Through the principles of empowerment, one intentionally shapes the culture for self-actualization, for production, prosperity, and the promotional growth of self and others.

There will be a community of confusion when learning environments do not use these principles or some intentional way of transforming the learned helplessness of our students.

On the severe side of environments that lack an active integration of these principles, there is no control in the learning space, resulting in chronic disruptions and significant safety issues. Even at the moderate level when a space does not systematically create an empowerment structure, one finds teacher burnout, grade-level promotion without grade-level mastery, and student attrition.

If we are not careful, the culture of empowerment can be limited to a behavior management program, as one of the ends to the methodology is to get a type of performance and behavior from students that is conducive to the lifelong journey to self-actualization.

But the culture of empowerment should not be reduced to behavior management, because this view implies that behavior in itself can be managed. Yet behavior is not a stand-alone entity in the lives of students (and in the lives of adults, for that matter). Behavior is the result of something greater than behavior itself.

To get at the heart of behavior, one must tap into the center of development. It is this aim to impact the root of behavior (which is in the sphere of psychosocial development) that mandates that we teach to the child and not limit empowerment to management.

The empowerment program gives us the tools for teaching to the child so that as educators (teachers, parents, and pastors) we are able to teach and effectively produce the results of empowerment: production, prosperity, and promotional growth.

By learning about power and experiencing power intimately, the empowerment model helps students produce, prosper, and promote growth in any environment (whether or not power is shared).

THE PRINCIPLES AND TENETS OF EMPOWERMENT

Empowerment is the instructional approach to teaching students how to self-assign power to achieve a life of production, prosperity, and promotional growth.

The statement above is the instructional framework of the empowerment philosophy. However, in short, the philosophy simply is grounded in the notion that self-actualization comes by way of accessed or generated power.

The seven principles of empowerment are ways to generate this power for self-actualization. While each principle is valuable in isolation, I believe a person must truly walk in all seven areas in order to be constituted as empowered.

It is important to note that an empowered person is not one who is simply powerful. As we know, being powerful may allow one to produce and even prosper but it does not necessarily promote the advancement of others.

Likewise, just because one promotes the advancement of others does not mean that they are able to promote their own advancement. As a result, there are many of us walking around proclaiming to empower others, yet we ourselves are living lives of limited production and prosperity.

The power that is generated from empowerment is about reaching a place where we can operate in all three domains of self-actualization. We are able to produce, prosper, and promote growth for ourselves and for others.

It is not enough for me as an educator to focus on the aim of an objective, but I also give special attention to the achievement of that objective. In saying this, let me say something that may contradict this statement.

Self-actualization can clearly exist as an aim. However, self-actualization as an achievement is a very difficult concept to reconcile.

Personally, I believe that our work on this earth is to self-actualize. It is to become the best self that one can be. For me, that means reaching a place where we have produced what we were required to produce. We have prospered in the areas we were to prosper. And we have promoted growth to the extent we were to promote it.

Unfortunately, the time in which we have accomplished those three areas concludes our work in the physical realm. It is at this time that our presence in the natural sense is no longer needed.

This discussion about the "physical realm" and the "natural sense" is definitely not leading into a discussion about the afterlife. No, I will leave that discussion for those who are equipped to handle the delicate and intricate nature of this belief.

The point that I am making, one that I believe I am authorized to make, deals with who we are while living and breathing the human experience. It is through this experience that we should be striving for the three Ps. When we have successfully fulfilled our work in these three areas, we have then simultaneously fulfilled our purpose for living.

So while we are striving for self-actualization, it is important to note that it is not about the destination of self-actualizing. It is about doing the work to get there.

In short, as long as we have breath in us, we should never sit back and rest on our laurels. There is always work to be done, and we should continuously strive to do it.

To say "I have self-actualized" and live in a world that is still growing and evolving is an oxymoron. While we are living, there is always something we can do. There are always places for us to grow. As a result, we are always in the state of self-actualizing.

I took some time to go into this discussion about life and death to really make a case that empowerment is not the end destination of self-actualization. No. Empowerment is about accessing, generating, and using power so that we can endure the process for self-actualization.

For an individual who claims to be empowered, he or she is saying that he is accessing, generating, and using power for the sake of his or her production, prosperity, and promotional growth.

For a person or a program that claims to empower, we are then saying that we are teaching others how to access, generate, and use power for the sake of their production, prosperity, and promotional growth.

The principles of empowerment deal with accessing, generating, and using power. In them, we learn that some power is within us as a skill and some power is in us as a thought process. We also see that some power is generated through our actions as individuals and some power is generated through our actions as a collective.

Because the work of self-actualization is a lifelong process, we cannot limit power to the principles of our choosing. Power generated by Innate Power (principle 2) is nothing if we do not have power in the area of Individual Responsibility (principle 5).

To be empowered so that we can produce, prosper, and promote growth, we need all of the seven principles: P^3 Commitment, Innate Power, Personal Assets, Global Efficacy, Individual Responsibility, Sense of Self, and Shared Accountability.

These are the power-generating principles of empowerment, and through them, we should teach and lead.

The empowerment model is not simply about having a belief system based on the seven principles. It is about employing systems and methodologies (what I refer to as tenets) that take the idea of empowerment from being an abstract concept to being a very real and tangible experience.

As I uncover the five programs of the SBC curriculum over the next six chapters, I will also profile how each of these principles was turned into tenets. I will show a systematic approach to these principles, not just in theory but in application.

But because I am sure you do not want to wait until you have read the entire book to get a clearer idea of the principles and their tenets, I will spend some time showcasing them in this chapter.

As you read, please know that these principles are beneficial for all. Regardless of the state of the person, having power that needs to better channeled for self-actualization or having no power at all, the empowerment model in its elasticity gives a very practical approach to connect with all people, even those who suffer from learned helplessness.

P^3 Commitment

The power that comes from P^3 Commitment stems from one's personal resolve to self-actualize. P^3 Commitment basically states that in order to self-actualize, we must be committed to the outcomes of production, prosperity, and promotional growth.

While we may not always act in accordance with the three Ps, we openly accept them as our aim and submit to the process of being held accountable (by ourselves and by others) for our behavior.

The principle of P^3 Commitment is a power source because it taps into the energy derived from motivation. It is not about ability, it is not about connections or resources, but it is about our thoughts, our attitudes, and our beliefs, which serve as the catalyst to how we show up in the world.

P^3 Commitment is the first principle, because without it power simply does not exist. One has to believe that he or she has the right to self-actualize before self-actualization can occur.

Where I am also a strong supporter of the idea of shared faith, where you can tap into the faith of others in the interim where faith is dormant or stagnant in your own life, I know that ultimate greatness does not stumble into our laps and it cannot be zapped down from the heavens.

Our mind, our thoughts, and the ideas that we hold to be true are a gift to man. No matter the state of the world around you and no matter how others choose to see you or respond to you, you have complete control over your thoughts.

Even if we have been conditioned to think a certain way, we ultimately must give permission for that conditioning to occur.

And in those unfortunate, but very real, circumstances when we have allowed someone to impact our outlook, we can still choose at any time to redirect our thoughts to a place that aligns with our truth.

Our thoughts are ours to use for good if this is what we choose.

And once you resolve to live a life of production, prosperity, and promotional growth, you commit to connect your expressions to this end. By aligning your thoughts, your attitudes, and your behaviors to this outcome, you create an energy field that causes others to recognize your potential (whether or not they admit or validate it).

The principle of P^3 Commitment is the first step to personal power. Here is where you acknowledge the right to self-actualize and you hold yourself accountable to the process.

The Teacher Tenet for P^3 Commitment

The teacher tenet for this principle is twofold.

- First, a teacher must always promote the ideas of self-actualization and the three Ps: production, prosperity, and promotional growth. Every experience in the classroom (or wherever the place of learning and growing exists) must connect explicitly and implicitly to this idea of personal greatness.

- Secondly, the teacher must connect the learner's behavior to the outcome of self-actualization. Through verbal acknowledgments and written documentation, the teacher becomes the secretary of the learner's P^3 Commitment. By doing this, the student begins to tap into the maturity and the wisdom of the teacher and begins to understand and differentiate specifically how some behaviors promote self-actualizations and then how other behaviors violate it.

It is important to note that the P^3 Commitment is not a rule. It is a principle. Therefore, the teacher can only provide opportunities for students to strengthen and fulfill this commitment. Only through student choice does it generate power. The job of the teacher is to track the behavior of students and create profiles for this commitment (or the lack of it).

If the student's profile demonstrates that he or she has not chosen to embrace the P^3 Commitment, then a decision must be made about the student's involvement in the empowerment program. The teacher (the school) can only control who is admitted into the program (we cannot control students' acceptance of empowerment).

Innate Power

Innate Power as a principle is similar to the P^3 Commitment in that it is something that exists within a person. While it can be strengthened and developed by way of experiences (simulated or natural), it originally comes from within the person who is on the road to empowerment.

In short, Innate Power is a person's natural right (and responsibility) for voice, choice, and dominion. In using one's voice, choice, and dominion, he or she can understand how power is used to produce results. Through these actions, power becomes personal.

To express one's self, to choose, and to take dominion is within each of us when we are born. As we grow, our Innate Power is either strengthened or weakened (and sometimes aborted) by the adults and institutions around us.

Innate Power can be viewed as an asset or as a threat, depending on the eye of the beholder. And how it is viewed will determine how it is fostered. As a result, how we are groomed to utilize (or suppress) our natural inclination to voice our ideas, to make our own choices, and to exercise authority in areas that belong to us, turns into personality traits in which we experience the world.

Voice, choice, and dominion do not have to be given to us in order to have power. But they have to be respected and developed.

The more we learn to use them for production, prosperity, and promotional growth, the more we are able to generate power for our own self-actualization.

The Teacher Tenet for Innate Power

> The teacher tenet for this principle deals more with the adult serving as the teacher than with the child serving as the learner. While the child may need some assistance to direct his or her Innate Power into endeavors that promote self-actualization, the real work of this tenet centers on the adult being able to share power (so that he or she can facilitate it).

> - The teacher must embrace that he or she does not exist as a supreme authority. While the teacher has responsibilities that center on the safety and the development of the students, the teacher must acknowledge that he or she too is human and is in process for his or her own actualization, and therefore, does not have ultimate control of power.
> - In order to facilitate the Innate Power of students, the tenet requires the teacher to submit to their power (in spaces that are safe and productive).

This teacher tenet is one of the most difficult tenets to enact (aside from Shared Accountability, where there is also a sharing of power between students and teachers). It takes a considerable amount of training (and support) to be able to implement this tenet, because it is such a nontraditional approach to how we separate the life stages of being a child versus being an adult.

Hopefully, by reading the rest of the book, readers will have a better understanding of this tenet. It typically is not the principle that causes the most discomfort. It is the application of the tenet that causes it. In chapters 2 through 7, I talk about how PSGL teachers shared power with students. Because they did a wonderful job, I believe the tenet of Innate Power will be a little easier to embrace.

Personal Assets

While the principle of Innate Power is difficult to absorb as a tenet, Personal Assets tends to be fairly easy to embrace as both a principle and a tenet.

Personal Assets is basically about what we can do and what we have. As a society, this is the typical fashion in which we already view and embrace power. From standardized test scores (which quantify our knowledge into a power source) to material possessions (which give us greater access to produce, prosper, and promote by way of our purchasing power), we already subscribe to the power generated by Personal Assets.

Personal Assets are divided into three categories: Internal Resources (skills and concepts related to reading, writing, math, science, and social studies), External Resources (technology, money, and human labor), and

Interpersonal Resources (analysis, autonomy, valuing, communication, and collaboration).

There is no question that Personal Assets can generate power. Therefore, an empowered person works to develop and employ these assets to achieve in his or her effort to self-actualize.

The Teacher Tenet for Personal Assets

Outside of the money and human labor aspects of Personal Assets, we have already been equipped with the methodology to teach within this tenet.

- Teachers must retain this principle of empowerment in their practice even when students struggle to obtain the learning objectives. I talk a lot in this book about the academic delays of disadvantaged students and the need to approach instruction unique to their learning needs. However, in no way have I or will I ever suggest that some objectives should be omitted just because there appears to be a deficit in retention. There is no question that students need to be able to read, write, compute, collaborate, communicate, and manage resources if they are to self-actualize.

- Teachers must also continue to showcase how Personal Assets generate power. Many times we get stuck with telling students they should do something from our perspective as adults without being able to demonstrate why they should do it from the perspective of being a child or a teenager. Just as we are not prone to following blindly, we really should not expect students to do so either. When teaching core learning objectives, this tenet emphasizes that the teacher integrates Innate Power and P^3 Commitment of students into the lesson. By doing this, the teacher will make learning relevant and therefore engage the students more effectively in the mission of building their Personal Assets. Personal Assets should not be about test scores. They should be about power. When put in the context of power (in a meaningful and authentic way), students will embrace the learning experience.

Global Efficacy

The principle of Global Efficacy generates power in that it gives the individual a worldly presence.

Limiting our existence to one of individuality and isolation does not allow us to use our talents to leave a legacy. Yet when we use our talent and our skills to advance the human experience, we give a piece of ourselves that goes beyond the physical realm.

As individuals, we are naturally social beings. How we come to be who we are has a great deal to do with the socialization process of our parents, our schools, our communities, and even with the visual messages we get from the media (and other social institutions). Through this socialization process, we become products of our society.

In short, being able to impact the world generates power because it has an exponential factor. When we help others, we expand our person. We become greater than self because we have committed to something that is outside of self.

Global Efficacy takes us beyond the impact that others have had on us and puts us in a position to have an impact on them.

The Teacher Tenet for Global Efficacy

> The tenet of Global Efficacy helps the teacher position the learning environment so that students learn their rights as agents of social change and fulfill their responsibilities to humanity. Through this tenet, students are able to see humanity on a scale larger than just their immediate environment. They are pushed to see regional connections between social problems, thereby seeing global solutions within a local context (having immediate value).

- Teachers must teach students about the socialization process and the ecological nature of social living. Students have a right to learn about their development as social beings, and they need assistance to see how events that happen on the other side of the world have a personal impact on who they are.
- Teachers must also allow students to become social-change agents in application, not just in concept. To do this, teachers must teach students how to be vigilant for social problems, how to take the initiative to develop social solutions to those problems, and how to act as leaders in mobilizing others for the sake of social change.

Individual Responsibility

The power of the principle of Individual Responsibility is in the respect that it garnishes for us as being a powerful person.

If we strive to be powerful for the sake of self-actualization and fail to fulfill our personal obligations, we become a threat to society. To keep our society moving in a way that is safe and productive, we need individuals who understand and support their social roles.

As parents, children, teachers, students, friends, citizens, and lovers we have responsibilities uniquely associated with each of these roles. And how well we fulfill them has an impact on the social relationships attached to those roles.

If we lived in a bubble, where we connected to others by way of a social relationship, we would be entitled to function exclusively according to the needs of those relationships. But we do not live in isolation. We very much are part of a social experience.

Likewise, power is only powerful when it is connected to something larger.

Let me restate that the power of empowerment is not just about personal gain. It is also about the personal advancement of others.

Therefore, when we seek to access and use power to self-actualize, we need to remember that actualization is ultimately not an individual endeavor. We need the respect and support of our fellow man to generate and use the power that truly belongs to the collective unit of society as a whole.

The Teacher Tenet for Individual Responsibility

The tenet of Individual Responsibility deals with the teacher's responsibility to give students credit for fulfilling their individual responsibility. Many times, we expect students to be responsible for social roles that we, as adults have assigned to them. We assume that students will understand and embrace these roles and therefore submit to the social obligations that we have assigned. When students fail to fulfill the duties assigned to those roles and often reject the role itself, they are penalized. This tenet directs the teacher (or the adult) to give credit when students fulfill their responsibility (instead of punishing them when they do not).

- The teacher needs to give academic credit for students' social fulfillment of their individual responsibility in a way that is systematic and consistent.
- The teacher should also assign academic credit in a way that is objective and not subjective.

Sense of Self

The principle of Sense of Self gives the individual power over himself and minimizes the power that others have over him.

When we know ourselves and accept ourselves for who are (and can differentiate that from our past, present, and future self), we are better able to position ourselves in situations that causes production, prosperity, and promotional growth.

There are five dominions to the sense of self (space, place, etc.), which allow an individual to understand and own his or her presence in the world. Through them, individuals do not have to wait for others to assign meaning to their person. They can assign it to themselves. As a result, individuals are liberated from the whims of others and can protect themselves from unhealthy relationships and situations.

The Teacher Tenet for Sense of Self

> The tenet of Sense of Self is simple in that teachers teach the five do-
> mains of self, give students time to reflect on the personal application
> of this principle, and allow for activities that will sharpen the principle
> as a skill and not just as a belief.

Shared Accountability

There is a lot of power in the principle of Shared Accountability. Basically, when you can hold yourself accountable, you limit the need for
someone else to hold you accountable.

But Shared Accountability generates power in other ways as well. Not
only do you generate power by limiting someone else's power over your
person, you also access more power in that you are able to use your
personal power for the accountability of others.

When there is an interchange of accountability, others are more responsible in how they handle accountability, and they are more involved
in fulfilling their own personal duties.

The Teacher Tenet for Shared Accountability

> The tenet of Shared Accountability is about creating systems that allow
> students to hold themselves accountable, as well being able to hold
> others accountable (including their teachers) in way that is democratic
> and safe for the community as a whole.
>
> - It is important to clarify that teachers cannot really hold students
>   accountable. Systems must hold students accountable. Our job as
>   teachers is to create a space where there are systems for accountabil-
>   ity. When students violate one of the seven tenets, they should al-
>   ready know the specific consequences and, as a result, be able to self-
>   assign the penalty.
> - It is also important for me to note that students must subscribe and
>   submit to systems of Shared Accountability in order to fully embrace
>   and maximize on the other tenets of empowerment. Empowerment
>   must be chosen, not mandated. It is learned and not forced. If stu-
>   dents do not choose to participate in Shared Accountability (or any of
>   the other tenets), they cannot partake in an empowerment-based pro-
>   gram.

Ultimately, empowerment is about power—not charity. You cannot have
an empowerment program without the tenet of Shared Accountability.

We must accept that violations to policies are likely to occur. It is
difficult for a person to transition into a place of being empowered (or to
maintain positions of power) without violating some type of social norm
or institutional policy. An empowered person understands this dynamic

juxtaposition of empowerment within a shared community and collaborates with others to define and to assign sanctions when systems have been compromised.

IN CLOSING . . .

I have personally come to understand that "empowerment" is not a lesson that can be taught by way of textbooks or lectures, projects or field trips, and not even by way of principles and inspirational teaching. It must be taught by personal example.

When we ask our students who come from disadvantaged backgrounds, or those who face a personal lifestyle that is in direct conflict to the principles that we teach, we have to be willing to show them how to be overcomers, how to transition from one state of being into the next, how to be empowered. We must make the lesson of empowerment come to life, in a real, up-close, and personal way. And the only way this can be done is when we allow ourselves to become living examples of what we teach.

Preparatory School for Global Leadership (PSGL) is a school that I started because I believed that I had a method, a way of teaching and learning that would empower the urban disadvantaged child. But as I sit back and think about it now, PSGL was a school that I started so that I could showcase empowerment to a group of students (and staff) who needed a real-life example of how to grow beyond one's current circumstances.

When I reflect on my journey of starting the school, I realize that every step along the way was personally teaching about empowerment. It is one thing to teach it, but it is another to live it. Unless we experience empowerment on a personal level, we cannot help students learn it, circumvent obstacles as they arise, and develop and employ the new skills needed to function to be empowered.

How can we get in the face of a student and push him or her to a place that is foreign and scary, asking him to become greater than his or her environment, when we ourselves have never become greater than our own environment? We can't. Why? Because we do not know what it looks like. We do not know what it feels like. Our role as a teacher becomes technical, causing us to miss out on the spirit of truly good teaching, where one teaches with relevancy, authenticity, and experience.

When I look at the faces of these students, I know that my process of starting the school was for them. When I became what I taught, when I empowered myself in spaces where there was no one there to empower me, when I chose to succeed without excuses, I became a living lesson.

These students saw me and our staff as extensions of the lessons we were trying to teach. Our lives, not by our perfection, but by our effort, showed students how to apply what we taught.

Because of this dynamic and our personal willingness to be transparent and share our stories, we created a school community of empowerment. We created a place where students combated traditional thought patterns on being (those that limited opportunities for greatness). We created a process for students to become activated in the academic process (instead of making it just the responsibility of the teacher). We created a place for students to produce, prosper, and promote growth. Please join me as I share with you how we empowered by way of the SBC curriculum. Through project-based learning, service learning, direct instruction, and student assessments and accountability, we taught about power and self-actualization by giving our students the power needed to generate power.

TWO

The Power of Project-Based Learning

Social Being and Change (SBC) became a formalized curriculum prior to the start of PSGL.

Taking signature projects from my time as a teacher, and graduate research from my studies in instructional leadership, I devised a school-wide model that would take empowerment beyond the realm of a single classroom experience.

Currently, there are a total of five programs in the SBC curriculum. However, the first two, Global Leadership Curriculum 7 (GLC7) and Leadership in Action: Self, School, and Society (LASSS), are the most central; they promote the key strength to the overall experience: global thought and individual power for urban learners.

It is with these two programs that students take on an identity different from traditional students. After experiencing GLC7 and LASSS, students act as school leaders, also transitioning the school to function as a social change agent.

The remaining three programs—Core Instruction, Institute, and P³ Advisory—position teachers and staff to ensure that responsibilities associated with schooling are met.

But SBC programming is ultimately not about schooling. It is about empowerment.

While empowerment can be a noble endeavor by other school and program leaders, not having the right curriculum can leave the ideas of empowerment dormant, resting on the papers on which they were written.

While we were a school—and that is where the strength of the last three programs of SBC curriculum come in to play (discussed in chapters 5 through 7)—this chapter and the next really speak to the heart of how

21

we employed empowerment among students who had typically been powerless in the schooling process.

Through it all, using both students and staff (including parents and partners), the seven principles and tenets of the empowerment model were activated.

This chapter, as well as the next five, showcases the instructional model of empowerment as a method, taking it well beyond the idea of being just a framework (as described in chapter 1).

GLOBAL LEADERSHIP CURRICULUM 7

The method of project-based learning (or PBL) is based on students learning important subject matter by engaging in self-directed projects. It is about allowing students to use their interest and their experiences to construct knowledge.

This concept of centering students in the learning experience so that they can create knowledge is called constructivism, and it was the theoretical umbrella to our entire program (not just PBL).

In empowerment, teaching is about giving power to students to produce, prosper, and promote growth. I believe this is constructivism at its best. Through the design of the curriculum and the work of the staff, students were able to produce.

When we used project-based learning, student took their experiences, their passions, and their interests to produce global solutions that would advance humanity.

GLC7, formally known as PBL7, was the project-based learning program used at PSGL. While it was only one of the five SBC programs, it was the one that received the most recognition.

Outside of our behavior management process, people were intrigued with how GLC7 worked. Associating student outcomes with this specific curriculum, I constantly received calls from other schools, educators, and partners on the design of GLC7 and how it could be reproduced.

While GLC7 was not the sole factor that empowered students, it did provide the most concrete application of the seven principles of empowerment. By engaging in a daily practice of self-directed exploration, students used all seven forms of power to create ways to advance the human experience.

The focus of the curriculum was to have students study global issues, develop and implement solutions, and then report their work to others so as to inspire further reform. Through seven concrete stages, students learned to think globally about personal problems and act locally to implement global solutions.

At the same time, they learned how to research, use technology, collaborate with others, and engage in critical scholarship using basic skills such as reading, writing, and math.

At the beginning levels, student learning was more focused on scholarship than it was on leadership. They learned how to manage the full demands of projects, dealing with problems associated with research, technology, and people, and at the same time they learned to work and negotiate timelines.

In the advanced levels, however, students moved beyond the more directed stage of the process. They learned how to be vigilant in their homes and in their community to identify personal problems. They learned how to develop and implement solutions (that were realistic, practical, and valid). And they learned how to ensure academic rigor by designing detailed projects that authentically met specific state standards.

I understand why our school gained recognition for our approach to project-based learning. It was amazing to see our "type of student" thrive in a method of thought leadership.

While our students struggled with gaining "proficiency" status on district-level tests, also having a track record of truancy and suspensions and a cultural experience of "learned helplessness," they were able to think critically about world issues, develop solutions, and work with high levels of power throughout the process.

GLC7 was academic rigor at its best, and all of our students participated in it. The seven levels provided a high degree of flexibility and elasticity, allowing us to engage students with different learning styles and temperaments.

Our special education students completed these projects. Our students who needed credit recovery completed these projects. And our students who were considered to be more advanced completed these projects.

Through instructional programming, students were supported through this unique way of learning and produced local solutions to global problems.

INSTRUCTIONAL PROGRAMMING

GLC7 can be classified and used in a number of ways. Primarily, we said it was a social studies and language arts curriculum because it significantly covered state level standards in each. However, when looking at district test results, it was our science scores where we were the most competitive.

It is possible to use the program to cover other subject areas or all the subject areas. Specifically, students explored issues that were grounded in one of the six social institutions experienced all around the globe (e.g., family, education, media, etc.). For each issue within a given global institution, students looked at the geography, the history, the economics, the politics, and the social dynamics of the problem.

It was natural for me, as a licensed social studies teacher, to ground the curriculum in social studies standards.

Incorporating language arts standards was also easy to do. As any social studies teacher knows, or even a math or science teacher for that matter, you cannot teach content without activating the writing process.

Because we wanted to showcase rigor, we had specific qualifications for the oral and written material (language arts) as well the content and how it was explored (social studies).

The unique thing about this curriculum was that it covered more than just social studies and language arts standards. As already suggested, the academic process for GLC7 included state standards in science as well as in math, art, and technology.

I celebrate this structure. Each and every project included six subject areas, all integrated into a thematic learning process. This approach made the topic being studied relevant and authentic.

GLC7 is very important for students who need a flexible approach to learning. Through the curriculum, students had more control over what and how they learned; as a result, they had more respect and applicable understanding for what and how they learned.

Program Component 1: The Schedule

GLC7 typically was executed during an instructional period called Project Block. During this ninety-minute block, students independently engaged in various stages of their projects, only using the staff (and their peers) as periodic resources.

Generally, Project Block was the first period of the day. As a result, the start of Project Block was like the start of a work day. Students were expected to sign in, they took part in a daily planning activity where they strategized their learning objectives for the day (even for those beyond Project Block), and they were to request necessary resources needed for their projects.

Students also took this time to request or schedule appointments with various personnel for specific reasons. If those requests were appropriate and if time was feasible, requests were granted and appointments were scheduled.

Project Block also allowed flexibility with other SBC programs. Some students contracted to use Project Block as Service Block (to be discussed more in the next chapter), therefore using the Service Block period in the afternoon for their Project Block.

For some students, GLC7 included two instructional periods. Whereas some students would negotiate to switch around their schedules, putting Project Block in the afternoon and Service Block in the morning, some students needed both periods to effectively carry out successful projects.

When students turned in their work at the end of the first period, a Project teacher would review them for baseline quality. If they did not meet basic quality standards, students were required to revise or complete their work in the afternoon.

In all, the schedule provided students with the necessary timing so that they would in turn learn how to manage their time. In addition, the schedule allowed for a great deal of flexibility necessary to meet the individual needs of each learner.

Program Component 2: Environmental Controls

Because the curriculum focus was just as intent on skills and processes as it was on content, the instructional environment for this curriculum was significantly different from that of traditional classrooms.

For GLC7, the work of the teacher was more about environmental control than instructional control.

Having up to thirty students in a group, you simply could not control the content and the process for each individual project. The richness and depth for each study was too much for a teacher to direct and develop on his or her own.

A partnership was required where students could control the content and the process while the teacher controlled the space in which they worked (ensuring its conduciveness for learning).

The environment consisted of individual work stations, computers with the Internet and critical software for performance, a lounge area for relaxation and mental reflection, as well as the bodies of thirty growing teenagers.

The tone of the room took on one of a library and the autonomy of students was that of doctoral candidates independently engaged in research.

To maintain the mission for student control and not teacher control, different staff members were assigned to staff Project Block room at various times of the day (or week).

I will discuss these different positions in the next section; however, here I want to explain the primary position and duty of the advisor who was charged with managing the environmental controls of the room.

There were three specific duties to managing the environment. First, the advisor was responsible for protecting the safety and well-being of each student. Second, he or she was responsible for ensuring that all resources (computers, Internet, projects, and project templates) were fully ready and accessible for the students' workday. Lastly, the advisor (or

whoever staffed the instructional period) was responsible for documenting the behaviors that promoted (or violated) the environmental vision
for the room (discussed more in chapter 7).

These three duties—student supervision, resource management, and
behavior documentation—were the primary function for ensuring a
smooth environment for GLC7 learning.

Program Component 3: Staffing

Environmental management was not the only duty associated with
successful GLC7 programming. Students also had to learn how to successfully navigate through the seven levels of the project, how to effectively use resources to complement the problem-solving process, and
how to master state standards that were incorporated to ensure academic
rigor.

First, we had a Project Block teacher. The person in this role was
responsible for the academic support, the environmental controls, and
the additional duties of involving parents and community members in
the process.

However, the work of incorporating students and families effectively
into this process actually stole time away from the actual academics. We
quickly discovered that the emotional demands of the population turned
these "additional duties" into the primary work of the Project Block
teacher, pushing the academics into more of a secondary position.

Simply put, the Project Block teacher was not enough for the needs of
our learners and the unique dynamics associated with successful GLC7
learning. As we grew to understand our students and our approach to
project-based learning, we learned how to staff differently.

In the more revised version of SBC programming, there are three
positions that perform the duties associated with GLC7. However, at
PSGL, we only evolved to use two of these people: a Project teacher (for
the academics) and an advisor (for the behavior).

Through an instructional period, our Project teacher provided instruction on the curriculum's seven levels, the state standards of the six subject
areas, and the use of resources (Personal Assets) to work autonomously
and effectively to receive credit for projects. While this weekly focus was
provided through our Institute program (chapter 6), we carved out an
additional period in the day strictly to promote academic rigor in our
projects. Our Project teacher (once known as the Project Block teacher) no
longer was responsible for managing Project Block.

The second position that emerged in the staffing transition process
was the position of the advisor. The advisor, who took over the management of Project Block, was responsible for the environmental controls for
project learning. In addition, with an added prep period, he or she was

responsible for building community (with students, families, and partners) for GLC7 and the empowerment model.

The Project teacher and the two advisors (for the middle and high school programs) really worked hand-in-hand to meet the needs of our students while ensuring the academic rigor in which GLC7 was designed.

Of course, there were other schoolwide systems that were employed to ensure project production and project performance (such as daily and weekly accountability systems). However, the real takeaway to this section is that GLC7, or any other project-based learning program, could not work without the consortium of people and systems structured to make it work.

EMPOWERMENT CONNECTION

While all five of the SBC programs address the seven principles and tenets of empowerment either directly or indirectly, there are only two that have a direct correlation with all seven: P^3 Commitment, Innate Power, Personal Assets, Global Efficacy, Individual Responsibility, Sense of Self, and Shared Accountability. GLC7 was one of them.

The P^3 Commitment

When students entered our program, they were faced with making a P^3 Commitment, and they understood how all five aspects of our program fostered this commitment.

At the door, we gave students permission to choose to be in our school (and we talked about the pros and cons of being at another school). We explained that by choosing our school, they had to commit to a disposition of production, prosperity, and promotional growth.

Just to ensure that students and parents really understood what we were asking of them, we required them to produce a baseline portfolio. A section of the portfolio required students to discuss a global problem and a solution. While we did not provide students with the seven-step format for this process, we did use the experience to connect students to GLC7.

As a result, GLC7 served as the first SBC program that students were introduced to. It was also the one in which they received considerable amount of training. In the first three months (which we considered their orientation/training period), students experienced a culture shock in how we defined schooling.

With the help of more seasoned students, GLC7 was the way in which we reminded them about the P^3 Commitment. Project-based learning at our school really required students to produce, prosper, and promote growth. GLC7 was very instrumental in helping students to embrace this mission.

Innate Power

Innate Power is a student's natural propensity to use voice, make choices, and have dominion. All three of these qualities came into play with GLC7.

First, students used their voice to articulate a problem. Through their voice, they explained what issues were important to them and why.

Second, students were able to make choices. They chose the standards that they wanted to incorporate into their study. They chose the ways in which they wanted to manage their projects. And they chose the solutions that they wanted to develop as answers to global problems.

Finally, students had dominion. They controlled their own workspaces. As long as their dominion did not interfere with the aesthetic appearance of the room or violate safety regulations, they were able to control how they would use their computer, their desk, and their file cabinet to their own satisfaction.

Student voice, choice, and dominion in projects actually overlap with each other. Where students had dominion, they also had choices. Where students made choices, they were also able to use their voice. And where students had voice, they usually used it to take dominion.

This ability to have personal power, and the comfort in knowing that it was respected and protected by the organization, made students feel a sense of personal pride.

I believed Innate Power is really what project-based learning is all about. It is why many students stayed. Learning was not about someone else's voice, choice, or dominion. It was about theirs.

There is nothing more authentic or more core than to incorporate something personal, something natural (something innate) into your work for production, prosperity, and promotional growth.

Personal Assets

The objective of Personal Assets was very strong in the GLC7 program. Although students worked independently to identify and solve problems, we still held them to a standard of quality.

It is through projects that students learned the value of reading, writing, and math skills (internal assets); research, technology, and human resources skills (external assets); and collaboration, valuing, and analysis (interpersonal assets).

GLC7 was a place where all three types of resources were developed and applied. Through this integrated approach to learning, students knew they had to sharpen these skills if they were going to be effective in their projects — if they were going to be successful at effecting change.

Global Efficacy

The theme of Global Efficacy requires the empowered person to pro-mote growth for others. Although students selected issues that were rele-vant to them, they designed solutions that really address the problem being studied (making the solution practical), solutions that had real-life value (making the solution valid), and solutions that were within the realm of their control to execute (making the solution realistic).

It was amazing to see teenagers transform from just being students to being social change agents. The longer students stayed in the program, the more vigilant they became in identifying social problems. If there was something that they saw on the news, something that they were experi-encing in their home life, or something that they wanted to learn more about, they used GLC7 as the vehicle for action.

The concepts of validity, practicality, and realism were a challenge to students, and they spent significant time thinking through appropriate solutions to problems. But they pushed through, often being very proud of their solutions and ready to take on the extended work of personal application.

Individual Responsibility

Individual Responsibility deals with making student responsibilities concrete. With Individual Responsibility, it is no longer a choice for stu-dents to take ownership of the duties and tasks associated with their lives. It is a requirement for empowerment.

This principle, highly connected with Innate Power as it respects the choices of students, holds them accountable for roles, positions, and as-signments that they have entered into.

GLC7 is phenomenal in how it connects this principle to urban stu-dents. Learning responsibilities associated with this curriculum looks dif ferent than with other program assignments.

A project can take anywhere from a couple of days to a couple of months (depending on the level of the project and the level of the stu-dent). While there are some restrictions to the total time allotted for com-pletion, there is still a lot of room for students to make choices based on their learning style and their interests.

At the end of the day, students understand that it is their responsibil-ity to complete a successful project regardless of how they have mapped out their work. When they find themselves facing challenges that they did not originally see, they must then find a way to problem solve.

Because there was a strong accountability plan assigned to GLC7 (by way of the P³ Advisory program, discussed in chapter 7), students knew they had to take their responsibilities seriously. They had to map out their work in a way that was realistic and reasonable. And they had to problem solve when they found themselves facing unforeseen challenges.

Because we were consistently there to hold them accountable, they experienced the real weight of individual responsibility. GLC7 was an authentic and safe way to teach this concept.

Sense of Self

Sense of Self was another principle that was directly addressed through GLC7. In this principle, students began to learn themselves on a deeper level.

One of the perspectives of Sense of Self is looking at how one produces versus how one performs. Separating the concepts of production and performance allowed students to see how they were able to work with timelines (for production) and provide meaningful solutions to global problems (for performance).

At the end of each week, students' work with GLC7 was presented in the realm of production and performance. During this time, students would reflect on the data and strategize ways to improve for the following week.

Another aspect of Sense of Self deals with space—areas of control and authority.

GLC7 teaches students about space by carving out and showcasing dominion for various players in the room. One of the systems required for GLC7 to work is to assign authority to students to control specific aspects of Project Block operations (discussed in chapter 3 in more detail).

A specific job could be to manage project files. Another student could be assigned to manage the questions of other students. And still another could be assigned to print projects and troubleshoot technical problems.

Regardless of the number of positions assigned, the students had to respect and honor the authority of their peers.

If a student wanted to reprint an assignment, he or she had to work with a peer to reprint it. If a student wanted to access stored files, he or she had to work with the peer who had the authority over the files. And if a student wanted to ask the teacher a question, the student had to get permission from the peer who was authorized to regulate the process.

Through GLC7's Project Block, we provided a democratic process for students to learn how to respect the space and dominion of others.

Shared Accountability

In order for any empowerment program to work, it must incorporate the principle of Shared Accountability and a system for it. Without Shared Accountability, all the other principles function as theories. They have no real teeth. It takes an accountability approach to make the other principles real.

Because of our respect for empowerment, however, accountability was rarely assigned. Instead, when students acted in a way that interfered with the vision or mission of the school, they typically were able to hold themselves accountable.

Through voice, choice, and dominion, students could participate in a discussion and identify a fair and suitable accountability sanction. Or they were able to just assign one, due to the effectiveness of the teacher in working with students to create accountability options before breaches occurred.

GLC7 was a good place for this principle/tenet to be activated. Because students negotiated their own timelines for projects, they also negotiated the outcomes. Through an honest discussion, students and staff determined what would happen if timelines were not honored. When students failed to meet those timelines, the consequences were merely part of the project, as they had already been spelled out.

TEACHER SHOUT-OUT

First, let me say that a "shout-out" is a way to give recognition to those who are important to us or to those who have made significant contributions.

This shout-out section is a way for me to acknowledge the amazing work of my teachers. Without them, my mission of empowerment would have been limited to the work I did in my classroom. Through their labor (and faith), however, the empowerment concept became a teachable model.

I owe a great deal of gratitude to every individual who came through the building. Each of them made a contribution. Even those who moved on, either because they did not believe in the mission or they did not have the capacity for it (emotional capacity or skill-related capacity), taught me through their struggles how to strengthen my approach to training.

Second, I want to clarify that all adults in the building were identified as teachers. Because we were a small staff in an open-space environment, we shared duties. We wore multiple hats.

Individuals who worked to organize the administrative files also worked to supervise students. Individuals who worked to serve lunch also worked to promote empowerment principles such as Innate Power (voice, choice, and dominion), Sense of Self, and Shared Accountability. Every adult worked with our students. If adults were in the building during school hours, they had a part in the mission.

As with all of the five curricular programs, it is really difficult to highlight the success of only one teacher. GLC7 was one of two central methods in our school; therefore, it was imperative for all individuals to be successful with this program

When I think of the evolution of GLC7 that I discussed earlier in the chapter, I feel the need to thank all of the individuals who played a part in our projects.

For some of you, it was more difficult than for others. But through all of you, we grew to have a much-respected project-based learning program.

Thank you.

STUDENT HIGHLIGHTS

Maurice, a sixth-grade student with severe behavior issues, settled long enough to come to school one morning with his own issue for exploration.

Typically, sixth graders worked within an issue selected by a teacher (students then selected their own problem from that issue). However, we believed it was important to allow Maurice to forgo the teacher-assigned project for the week so that he could work on this project he was so obviously excited over.

We had just had a snow day, and I guess Maurice had sat at home and thought about the different impacts of snow. When he came to school, he said, "I want to do a project on how snow affects people with jobs."

What can you say to a child who lives in a home where neither parent works and from my understanding never had worked a traditional job for any substantial period of time? You almost want to run and champion any activity that gets him thinking about employment.

So with this opportunity, we helped Maurice devise a Snow and Work project. The way the project was designed, Maurice looked at statistics on snowfall in Milwaukee. He examined the pros and cons of various transportation systems during a snowstorm. He even looked at the relationship between employment rates and quality of living in a given city.

Maurice received social studies credit because he learned how to read and analyze graphs and charts. He received math credit because he had to calculate numbers in order to perform the analysis related to unemployment rates and snowfall accumulation.

He received science credit because he looked at the properties within salt that allowed it to function as a dissolving agent for snow and how these same properties affected asphalt. He received language arts credit because (of course) he was required to use Standard English to present his work in written form.

Now, this learning experience may not seem involved for some, but I did not tell you that Maurice also had an IEP (Individualized Learning Plan) giving him the label of being a special education student. With this, he was significantly delayed in his reading, writing, and math skills, to the extent that in grade 6, he was only functioning as a second grader.

I am not going to say that through this project, Maurice was totally transformed and became a serious student. No, Maurice was Maurice. But Maurice did buckle down to complete this particular project. It was his. He came up with the idea. He (with our help) designed and completed it.

During the portfolio assessment at the end of the year, Maurice sat in front of a panel of community assessors and clearly articulated what he learned from the project.

Maurice really did not have a completed portfolio, but he showed up at the assessment to talk about his Snow and Work project.

The assessors on the panel—an instructor from a local college, a loan officer from a local bank, and a police officer—were really impressed by the project and his passion for it.

Through GLC7, students were able to make connections such as these, where school became a place for them to think critically about their own lives and experience scholarship in a way that was inviting and not intimidating. It was a way for all students, even students like Maurice, to experience success.

IN CLOSING . . .

Our project-based learning program received significant attention because of its design, rigor, and impact on our student population. There are a lot of PBL schools that use a student-centered format to learning, in which students identify and develop their own projects.

However, GLC7 was different in several ways.

First, there was a scaffolding of student projects to make them grade-level specific or learning-style appropriate. Other PBL programs focus on the project as a whole and do not give room for the different developmental needs required to complete a successful project.

The second difference was that we assigned responsibility to our learners to learn. Because it was their responsibility to engage in learning, just as much as it was our responsibility to facilitate it, students were held accountable for doing their part.

We did not allow them to "discover" this lesson on their own, as some schools claimed to have done. While there is merit in allowing students to experience the full ramifications of poor decisions (such as failing a grade or dropping out of school to later come back and get a GED), I did not believe our students could successfully rebound from this lesson.

Some decisions can be so poor that they send students to places where the impact becomes lifetime baggage, making it almost impossible to recover.

While we championed student choice, we also believed that some choices were not within students' dominion to make.

Students had a choice: to enter our program or to attend another school. If they were in our classrooms, they participated in the work associated with GLC7. It was OK for them to choose how they would complete projects, but it was not OK for them to choose to fail.

They had to attend another school to make that decision.

THREE

Service Learning and Empowerment

Service learning is a teaching method that allows instructional objectives to be met by engaging students in service activities.

If a math teacher wants to teach a student about percentages, this teacher may negotiate to have the student work one day a week in a neighborhood convenience store. There, the student could manually determine the tax to be paid by using the proper percentage to calculate the amount.

If a science teacher wants to teach a student about different animal species, this teacher may have the student work one day a week at a zoo or an animal shelter. There, the student could learn to care for animals by learning and appreciating the needs of their species.

There are endless ways that you can incorporate service in the instructional process so that students can get an up-close-and-personal view of the subject matter.

The value of service learning is that it allows for active learning. It is not passive, as students are not simply sitting at a desk in order to receive and store information. Instead, they are actively using their brain, their senses, their body, and their emotions (the entire person) to learn.

At PSGL, service learning was the second core of SBC programming for teaching empowerment (along with project-based learning).

As with all schools, students were expected to learn; however, through SBC, students at PSGL were expected to learn a certain way (according to the vision).

Most of our students had never been so present in the academic process. Getting them engaged in learning and then teaching a totally new methodology for learning really required them to work. It was this experience of work that constituted the first aspect of the service learning program.

The second aspect of the service learning program dealt with operational leadership. All of our students—100 percent—had an operational role in the school's program. If students were enrolled in the program more than ninety days (the time period designated for their training), they were activated as leaders.

Our objective was to provide an active way to teach about the seven types of power (as relating to empowerment). Therefore, all the students served in some type of operational capacity: as an administrator, technician, manager, developer, organizer, ambassador, or speaker.

In theory, who can really have a problem with our service approach to empowerment? However, when you look more holistically at our work and how we gave power to a group of students who were not familiar with having power, a lot of questions can surface.

I guess if we wanted, we could have tried to limit or control empowerment so as to not let it get out of hand. But when you activate the learning environment as a place for empowerment, you open the doors to a set of dynamics not easily understood.

To empower students is to empower them. You cannot turn it on and off. We could not tell students they were empowered one minute and in the next say, "We are not doing empowerment right now." It either is or it isn't.

And this is where it gets tricky.

I think it would be easier to understand the challenges if I first paint a clearer picture of our student population at PSGL.

I have already stated that our students came from disadvantaged backgrounds. In fact, 90 percent of our students came from this background. Because of this high percentage rate, we were classified as a Title I school.

According to research, students living in poverty face greater risks of dropping out of school, being teenage parents, and entering a life of crime.

Prior to PSGL, I would have argued this notion on poverty and risk (especially since my grandmother raised all seven of her children in extremely impoverished conditions, yet none of them dropped out of school, became teenage parents, or entered a life of crime).

But working in an environment where the emotional and physiological challenges of poverty tried to define the African American experience of our students (our student population was also 98 percent Black), I have had to reexamine my views on race and poverty.

Most of my work in urban disadvantaged schools consisted of working with minority students in general. I have been fortunate enough to work in schools where there was a nice balance between Black, White, Latin, Asian, and Native American students.

But at PSGL, everyone looked like me (except for my staff, which I tried to keep as diverse as possible).

So when I was faced with the emotional energy of sadness, anger, fear, and confusion that permeated our building and the pervasive state of hunger, fatigue, and sickness, as an urban African American, I had to fight against the resignation that this phenomenon defined the Black experience.

While I still believe there is a difference between poverty and generational poverty (where learned helplessness is extreme), I do embrace poverty (not race) as a factor causing our students to be a very difficult group to teach.

Race and poverty were not the only elements we had to figure out. We also had to learn the work of a sizable special education population (8 percent to 17 percent) and learn to exist within the restrictions of our funding challenges (at best, receiving 75 percent of state dollars given to the district to provide public education).

While I talk more about these numbers and their challenges in chapter 8 ("The Politics of Empowerment"), I do want to make a case for the unusual work we subscribed to when we set out to activate empowerment in a school of high student needs and limited funding.

It was difficult for some staff to understand why we went through so much trouble to give power to students who seemed to need other things first (such as food, counsel, and traditional programming). And when times got turbulent, as they often did in the beginning, I too questioned if these students were right for the empowerment program.

But these students, being so disenfranchised from the learning experience, needed something that was going to pull them in. They were already exposed to remediation, government interventions, and charity hand-outs—why would we not try something different?

Through redefined scholarship and operational leadership, school took on a new meaning for our students. Instead of changing students to embrace our standard of schooling, we changed schooling to embrace them.

While the other four programs of the SBC curriculum expose students to empowerment, service learning fully activated it. As a result, accessed and generated power became one of the key catalysts that changed the paradigm of the powerless.

LEADERSHIP IN ACTION: SELF, SCHOOL, AND SOCIETY

Service learning was designed to work side by side with project-based learning at PSGL. While there are areas of overlap, these two programs exist as two separate units. Whereas Global Leadership Curriculum 7 (GLC7) provides the framework for global leadership, Leadership in Action: Self, School, and Society (LASSS) provides the framework for local leadership. The two work together to help students produce, prosper, and promote growth in self and in others.

Initially, service learning was intended to only serve as a leg for GLC7. It was at the advanced stages of GLC7 that students implemented their global solutions at the local level. This implementation was how service was designed for our school.

After studying our students, we quickly discovered that students needed more structure and training for local-level implementation of their global projects.

As a result, a separate service learning program was formed, creating a space for training and structure beyond what was provided through GLC7. As a separate unit, service learning established a foundation for leadership by strengthening students' disposition for empowerment.

With three different parts, students led in areas that related to self (personal leadership), school (program leadership), and society (community/global leadership). By providing service in all three areas, students developed skills associated with effective leadership and ultimately prepared to enter into the advanced stages of project-based learning for global change and a life of personal empowerment.

In part one, the Personal Leadership division, students received service credit for their daily function as student leaders.

Students fulfilled the vision in periods that would be traditionally viewed as nonservice time. When coming to and from school and when in group social settings such as lunch, students functioned as leaders.

In part two, the Program Leadership division, students worked to make contributions to our school's operation. Whether it was in how we incorporated visitors into our building, how we managed the lunch system, how we hired and trained new staff, or how we marketed our curriculum and recruited new students, all of our students had a significant role to play in the success of our program.

Finally, in part three, the Community/Global Leadership division, students worked outside of the building to serve others in their local and global communities. Through this division, students worked at community organizations such as the House of Peace, Salvation Army, or Plymouth Manor Nursing Home. They also worked in the advanced stages of their projects (GLC7) by developing and implementing local solutions to global problems.

For the five years we were in operation, our program for service was loosely called service learning. Once the school opened, my work as director/principal/teacher did not allow me to work the curriculum as I had done prior to the start of the school. While I continued to strengthen the instructional delivery of SBC, systems and activities that evolved were not formally named as LASSS until now.

As a result, service learning at our school was the least developed as a curriculum program but it was the most active. I am sure that my work over the past year in strengthening SBC will take the accomplishments discussed in this chapter to the next level.

I am pleased in what we were able to do with our loosely defined service learning model. Although new in name, everything discussed in this chapter existed as an aspect of our program.

INSTRUCTIONAL PROGRAMMING

Because service learning was not about textbooks and teacher instruction, programming for leadership could not be limited to a class. As stated before, the entire school day was structured to serve as a platform for leadership.

First, we created daily schoolwide systems that positioned students to perform as student leaders even when they were just functioning as students.

Secondly, we manipulated a schoolwide schedule to create a routine for some of our service learning activities. These routines simplified the dynamics of service learning, making it more manageable and, essentially, more effective.

Finally, we redefined staff positions so that responsibilities associated with service learning were mandated duties and not an extension of good teaching (left to the whims of teacher choice).

Because we could not turn student empowerment on and off, we had to be prepared to embrace it all day. Through schoolwide systems, schoolwide scheduling, and schoolwide staffing, we were properly prepared for the all-day affair of service learning.

Schoolwide Systems

So much of what we ask from students on a daily basis requires personal leadership. Aside from the simple fact that we are constantly asking students to set good examples for their peers and their siblings, there is a long list of things we ask students to do that they do not want to do (no matter how logical it is for us, as adults).

In doing this, we typically have them dismiss their feelings for the things they want to do (as a result, invalidating a very fundamental place of their being).

As teachers, parents, pastors, and concerned neighbors ("the village") responsible for the care of children, we all do this. We have them do things that we know are good for them, regardless of whether they see it this way or not.

This disregard for the desire and vision of young people bothered me when I was a child. And it still bothers me, as an adult charged with the responsibility of taking care of children.

I am not suggesting that we simply let students do what they want to do because it feels good to them. But I do believe that they should get credit for doing the work that we ask of them. As those of us who are employees know, it is not always easy to do something when directed, especially when it appears to have no value.

So at PSGL, schoolwide systems allowed us to give students credit for following our direction. We understood that it took personal self-control and personal leadership to fulfill many of our obligations.

For each day students managed their person so as to fulfill the mission for student empowerment, they received a score card point (service learning credit).

This point system was specifically a part of our schoolwide behavior management system. For each class period, even lunch and dismissal, teachers documented students for the choices they made (more about this system to come in chapters 6 and 7).

When students acted in a way that represented the school's vision, such as engaging in the contractual handshake for teaching and learning, assisting a peer with either homework or emotional management, or writing a note to a teacher to express a concern instead of blurting it out, this behavior was tracked (and eventually scored).

Likewise, when students acted in a way that violated the school's vision, such as arguing with a teacher, not coming to class with required supplies, or violating someone's personal space, this too was tracked (with no opportunity for points).

Through our nightly tracking system, where documentation from all teachers was pulled together, we were able to identify those students who had good days ("good" as it related to our mission). This core system, a culmination of several smaller schoolwide systems, allowed students to receive their daily points and ultimately receive service learning credit for their personal leadership.

Schoolwide Scheduling

The other way we programmed for service learning was by creating a system where service learning activities became routine. First, we had Service Block, which was the fourth block of the day. In Service Block, students worked with individual staff members to perform duties associated with school operations.

The other way we worked with the schedule to allow for service learning was by creating a four-day week. Mondays through Thursdays were designated as instructional days; weekly objectives were introduced on Monday and then tested on Thursday (discussed in more detail in chapter 6).

Fridays were considered field days. Three Fridays out of the month, students would engage in group field activities. In teams, they would go out into the community to provide group service.

On the first Friday, however, we approached field work differently. Because these days were designated as our monthly professional days, we required students and their families to work together at home to provide individual service to the community. There was a specific framework from the SBC curriculum that was used, guiding students and parents to make three monthly service connections with rotating social institutions.

Schoolwide Staffing

Every adult in the building had to become a service-learning supervisor. In this role, they had to find ways for students to assist with the duties and responsibilities of their work.

While some may think this requirement was good for the staff because it provided them some help, I want to clarify that being a service learning supervisor provides more work for the supervisor than help from the students.

Not only were teachers and staff required to do the standard work associated with their roles, but additional work was created when they stepped into the position of service learning supervisor. It required a great deal of creativity and planning to devise meaningful program leadership opportunities.

There were systems, however, put in place within the instructional program to support staff as service learning supervisors.

First, the behavior management plan was very helpful for the Personal Leadership component of LASSS. Because it was so detailed and methodical, teachers did not have to do any additional work in order for students to receive service-learning credit. The data already collected for behavior management was simply transferred into a student scorecard and shared as part of the service-learning program.

To help teachers provide "school" leadership for students, we would sit down in our monthly meetings and collaborate together on how to effectively incorporate students into operational roles. We would take a list of the entire student body and identify those students who had naturally evolved into taking on leadership.

During those times, we would identify students who were overused. Typically, these were students who were natural administrators or support staff. They made their way into those positions without our direction. We actually had to work hard to not use them. Not only were they available for these positions, but they were actually quite good at them.

Next, we identified those students who did not have a special role. We discussed their strengths and weaknesses and brainstormed how those students could be best utilized. We collaborated as a team and helped each other institute school leadership positions for all of the students.

ADDITIONAL PROGRAMMING: ACTIVATING THE PRINCIPAL

The instructional programming for schoolwide systems, schoolwide schedules, and schoolwide staffing generally made the work for service learning quite manageable.

But unfortunately, for 10 percent of our student population, this programming was not enough.

While all students, regardless of their level of difficulty, were expected to participate in the personal and global leadership aspects of the program, it was a bit more challenging to include all students in operational leadership.

There were times when teachers were not able to incorporate the more difficult students of an already challenging population into an operational role at the school. Even though they sat down to discuss ways for all students to be get involved with operations, teachers still walked away from the table with some students not having a special assignment.

So I took on the job.

For the first few years (until I was able to strengthen my approach to training), I served as the service learning supervisor for those difficult students.

When I was not in those placement meetings, I could generally predict the students for whom staff would genuinely not be able to create a position.

Frankly, these were the students who did not have the disposition for administrative or support work. Their dispositions were too entrepreneurial for routine work and support positions. They were not keen on the idea of following someone else's lead, and they had no qualms about letting you know how they felt. As a result, they were left at the bottom of the barrel.

So I took them.

I knew these students well. They were ones that I connected with the most, as many of them reminded me of me. When one does not fit into the status quo or into someone else's paradigm, it is very easy for one to get labeled as difficult.

Because for the most part I was that difficult student—and even sometimes that difficult staff member—working with these students was an opportunity for me. Through the work, I was able to show the strengths of all students even when they thrived on existing outside of the box.

These students were not all neat and tidy, they were not traditional and conventional, and they definitely were not meek and submissive. But that does not mean that they needed to be stuck with a label and alienated from empowerment.

I do not think "disrespectful" students want to be disrespectful. They are disrespectful because that is how we label their behavior. I do not think "defiant" students want to be defiant. They are defiant because that is how we label their behavior. And I definitely do not think "difficult" students want to be difficult. Again, they are difficult because that is how we define them.

And because *we* have labeled them as disrespectful, defiant, and difficult, we cannot see the leadership potential in them.

So relating to these students and seeing true value in the areas of leadership, I received the honor of working with them. And because of my job as the school's director/principal, students worked with me in the areas of executive leadership, where they served in roles related to public relations, student discipline, and staff training.

When I activated these students in my work with public relations, they truly became my allies. They were like miracle workers as I went out to promote our program or to request funding. If you have experienced a "difficult," "defiant," and even a "disrespectful" student, you know they have a boldness that is not easy to come by.

These students were very comfortable with public speaking because for the most part, they loved the attention, they loved speaking their mind, and they loved to tell the truth about who they really were and what they really needed.

In addition to speaking engagements, I also involved my students in student discipline. When a student who typically gets into trouble sits down and coaches a mild to moderately behaved student, the "difficult" student becomes a role model. Ironically, their influence on other students shifts to a positive one, as opposed to the negative one they had when left in the traditional role of fighting with their teachers.

These "difficult, defiant, and disrespectful" students are incredible in being able to see both sides of a situation and then mediating a win-win solution. Having sat in the principal's office most of their school career, they have been indirectly trained in the definition of appropriate behavior. They just have not been in a position to be "appropriate" in a way that is natural for them.

When having to deal with a discipline issue, I would give the student "in trouble" the option of resolving the conflict the traditional way (which usually meant a detention or suspension) or the nontraditional way (which meant negotiating with one of the student leaders—those perceived by teachers as being "difficult"—to negotiate a corrective action plan).

Ninety percent of the time, students opted for the nontraditional approach, allowing my student leaders (the hard-core difficult ones) to serve as advisors.

The discipline work of my student leaders had two functions. First, they helped create a corrective action plan with the student in trouble. Then, they worked with me on finding ways to modify the classroom so that these students would not get into trouble.

Finally, these "difficult" students-turned-student-leaders were very instrumental in staff training. For whatever reason, these students had a strong need for justice and could easily see when there were teacher gaps in empowering students.

My student leaders loved the idea of active empowerment; therefore, they championed it. So when teachers, usually new staff in training, would violate the principles or the structure for student empowerment, my student leaders would let me know via notes.

I have to be honest, though. It took time to train students on the power of written documentation. Many times they would want to verbally attack the gap and have the teacher immediately repent and repair the damage. I had to work hard to teach them that this process was not conducive for the learning environment, and it was not fair for the teacher who needed to be supported in the training process.

Because my student leaders, the "difficult" students, embraced and pioneered note writing as a system to deal with instructional breaches, note writing became the way at our school. Whenever a grievance surfaced, this was the method for resolution.

As with the other students, the additional programming allowed the 10 percent to become a part of operational leadership. Just as other students had a natural disposition to fulfill administrative and support roles, my student leaders had a natural propensity to lead and direct others.

The alternative service learning work provided through my executive leadership gave room for them to lead. They had a place at our school in that their natural self—everything that we label as disrespect, defiance, and difficulty—was truly used to support our operations for student empowerment.

EMPOWERMENT CONNECTION

As was the general nature of the SBC curriculum, one could argue that the design and implementation of LASSS allowed for all seven empowerment principles to come to life. Yes, there is an undeniable connection with LASSS and the P^3 Commitment, Personal Assets, and Global Efficacy. But I think the true spirit of LASSS lies within the principles of Innate Power, Individual Responsibility, Sense of Self, and Shared Accountability. No other curriculum program can impact students in these four areas the way that LASSS did.

Innate Power

SBC's service learning program was an incredible way to assign power to students at PSGL. However, the brilliance was in how it addressed the need to use Innate Power as a power source for self-actualization. Not only did students have access to shared power provided by the courtesy of school personnel, but they were able to generate personal power by the use of their voice, choice, and dominion.

In chapter 2, the discussion of project-based learning, I gave a good amount of attention to voice and choice as elements of internal power. However, I would like to draw special attention to dominion, the third area of internal power, and the special place it has within service learning.

Service learning allowed our students to experience dominion beyond the aspect of being able to manage their own workstations.

The empowerment model supports a very natural inclination that we have as people to control, to protect, to fight for, and to manage. So through it, dominion was broken down into two areas: assigned authority and shared authority.

In assigned authority, students have complete dominion in a particular area. They were given something that only they could manage, or they were assigned to a position that only they could staff.

In either case, that process or that possession was theirs. And they proudly claimed all rights to owning it.

In shared authority, however, students worked together to collectively meet an objective. It was understood that a partnership was the only way the work could be completed.

Although a shared effort, the partnership was still highly defined and structured. Only those people who officially rallied together for the objective could have influence. It was not open for newcomers unless the group agreed to expand their sphere of dominion.

Through assigned and shared authority, students had control over a particular area. Now, just because they had dominion does not mean that they were not accountable to others in their areas of authority. We definitely instituted an accountability program to balance their authority (this is discussed more in the Sense of Self section of this chapter).

But aside from accountability, students felt stronger when they were in a position of influence. They were able to see themselves as powerful in that through their authority, their creativity, and their labor, they were able to affect outcomes.

Individual Responsibility

Being a student is a responsibility assigned by the law. It entails going to school every day on time, turning in medical excuses when out sick, and fulfilling the obligations of the assigned grade level so as to get promoted to the next.

In the Personal Leadership division of LASSS, students received credit for fulfilling these duties—the duties associated with being a student.

In short, traditional schooling does not credit students for this role. They assume that students come to the table naturally respecting the law, with an inherent desire to fulfill these duties.

For the most part, this is naive thinking. How many adults want to get up and go to work every day? Yes, there are those of us who truly enjoy our jobs. However, if money were not an issue, the general consensus about employment and working would be different. We would define our work truly based on our interests, our work style, and our needs.

To expect students (especially those dealing with learned helplessness) to function each day outside of this paradigm is unfair. School is usually not about their interest, their work style, or their immediate needs. It does not matter that we work hard to reform the schooling process or campaign to persuade students that schooling is for their ultimate good. There are duties and expectations that students simply must fulfill, not because they want to but because they have to. It is the law.

LASSS allowed students to get credit for meeting state mandates in areas such as attendance, immunizations, and acceptable behavior (as defined). It was our way at PSGL of acknowledging the effort that was required to produce in ways that someone else has dictated.

Sense of Self

Part of Sense of Self centers on understanding the areas of dominion that are within your control and those areas that are not. While Innate Power is in all of us, there are limits. The tenet of Sense of Self teaches students how to respect these limits and provides guidance for how to appropriately activate their voice, choice, and dominion.

Because our students had authority (assigned and shared), they typically did not have to fight for it. It is the fighting for power that sends many of us into places that really are not within our control. While we are busy fighting for power, we cannot see when we really are outside of our jurisdiction.

In our service learning program, students learned to respect the dominion of others. While students entered into the program with a huge complex against authority, giving them power to have dominion in a particular area allowed them to view authority differently.

They learned that sometimes when in authority, you have to take action that is unpopular. They learned that sometimes when in authority, you make mistakes. Because you are so focused in one area within your domain, it is easy to overlook other areas.

Finally, they learned that sometimes you need others to follow (even when they do not agree with your leadership), because it is the only way to demonstrate the effectiveness of your decision.

These lessons became vividly real as students encountered them in their leadership. Once they experienced these difficulties, they were able to respect others as they too wrestled with them. They learned that these challenges were associated with the realm of authority, and it no longer was personal. It was just the business of leadership.

Shared Accountability

I have already said that empowerment is a concept that needs to be taught by way of example. Such is the case with accountability. If we truly want to teach students about being accountable, we need to give them a visual. We need to show them that accountability is safe, and we need to model how an empowered individual is just as comfortable holding others accountable as they are comfortable with being held accountable in a collective community.

Because our service learning program positioned students and staff as partners, it was a natural place for this philosophy to come to life.

When the level of personal power increased with students, as did their comfort with school leadership and their confidence with school ownership, so did the publicity of teacher mistakes.

In a traditional school, the glitches of teachers are easy to cover up, as students are not as aware of operational and instructional policies. Yet students at PSGL knew policies because they promoted them. And when a teacher failed to follow the rules (either by intent or neglect), students, fortunately or unfortunately, were able see this.

For this reason, Shared Accountability through service learning was more for teachers than it was for students. We trained the teachers on how to handle the humanness of leadership. When mistakes were made, we encouraged the adults to be forthright about it. As often as the teacher could turn shortcomings into teachable moments, the less difficult it would be for him or her to embrace the notion of Shared Accountability.

There were some matters that were dealt with privately when operational gaps occurred; however, for the most part, we had a school climate where students and staff were able to dialogue about problems and work together to create solutions.

It was easier to share the work of a successful school by sharing power than it was to fight with students about having a successful school because we, as adults, withheld power. That approach seemed to be counterproductive.

Through LASSS, students and staff both worked systems and processes so that accountability became a community affair and not an individual war.

TEACHER SHOUT-OUT

Although I will single out one teacher below, I would like to state for the record that it is hard to single out a specific teacher in this section. Every last one of them, regardless of how long they stayed in the program, need to be recognized and celebrated for how they supported the tenets of empowerment in our service learning program.

From the moment our staff interviewed for the job through the ways in which they were trained and eventually worked side by side with students, they had to be willing to share power.

In order to empower students, they chose to give up some of theirs.

I know this was not easy for many of them. And honestly, I believe I was fortunate. I was able to find individuals who believed in student empowerment so much that they were willing to put themselves in uncomfortable positions to promote the concept.

It is one thing for me to promote empowerment, as this is my methodology. It is a concept that has been with me personally from childhood.

But it is another thing entirely for someone else to come along and promote it. He or she simply must have an open mind and a willingness to interact with students in a different way.

And that is what the staff at PSGL was all about. Through them, the model for empowerment came to life. In their willingness to grow in order to support the growth of our students, they gave legs to my mission.

To make my point clear of how awesome the teachers were, let me talk about how the staff shared power with students. Our most effective process was through a system we used for hiring new teachers. In this process, students worked with other students, even our staff, to identify and bring new staff into our program.

When new teachers interviewed for the program, part of the process included a mock lesson along with a student interview.

For twenty minutes, candidates would teach, and then for the remaining ten minutes, students would ask questions. We trained students about the role of interviews and the techniques of interviewing.

Not only did students ask questions, but they also completed a rubric where they evaluated the strengths of the applicant. When all interviews were complete, the students got together to discuss the candidate of their choice. From this discussion, they made a student recommendation for hire.

Most of the time, students and staff were on the same page with their recommendations. As a result, when a teacher was hired, the students believed it was their recommendation that led to the new hire. This made the students feel really empowered, as they believed that they were not just students, they were truly leaders.

Sometimes, our students took this shared dominion too far (smile). When a teacher that they recommended later imposed some type of disciplinary action, it was not unusual to hear students say, "That's why we should not have hired you!" Or when students felt like teachers were misusing their power, we would hear students say, "We hired you, we can also fire you."

Our staff actually absorbed the nature of these words for what they were, not for what they appeared to be. Students had really embraced their roles as school leaders and were relishing their right to be more than just a student.

As I write this, I am smiling to myself because I can see some of my colleagues vehemently rejecting the idea of tolerating such words from students.

But I guess in order to appreciate this experience, one would have to value the sticky idea of giving students power in order to teach it. And in its stickiness, one would have to believe that the ends justified the means.

When students felt as though they truly had power, we were able to leverage this feeling in situations when they acted powerless. It was easier to talk to students about their responsibilities when they did not feel victimized and were actually allowed to serve as leaders.

And it would be naive, if not simply wrong, to think that students would walk in this new place of authority without fumbling with power.

This was the fortunate asset that I had in my staff. Through their willingness to walk side by side with students and to embrace the developmental nature of learning how to have and use power, empowerment was very much an active part of our culture. It was not something we just talked about. Thanks to my staff, it was something that we lived.

Mrs. McIntyre

I do want to take a moment to recognize Mrs. McIntyre. She worked for PSGL in our second and third year of operations. Even when she physically left the building (and also the city), she stayed in contact. Spiritually, she was still joined to the mission. Her commitment, her drive, and her integrity had a lasting impact on the development and operations of our school.

Mrs. McIntyre's story with our school is a little different from the stories of the other teachers mentioned in this book. Whereas other teachers were recognized for their mastery of specific instructional methods, it is important for me to recognize Mrs. McIntyre for the way in which she personally modeled the principles of empowerment.

It is one thing to teach a principle and another thing to live it. This was the work of Mrs. McIntyre. She served as living curriculum for the service learning process.

It is very important that as adults, we recognize the impact that the unwritten curriculum has on our youth. There is no doubt about it. We teach when we are not trying to teach. How we live our lives showcases what we really believe. If we are honest, we often teach (or lead students) with a gap in our lessons. We say one thing, yet we do something else entirely different.

I am not suggesting that Mrs. McIntyre was a saint or that she was perfect. She really did wrestle with her cultural understanding of our students and the community in which we served. She had to be willing to see a world bigger than the one she had when she entered our program. She had to have a better understanding of herself and come to know her own purpose as a practitioner and as a person. And she had to be willing to redefine power so that she could effectively participate in the service learning aspect of our program.

So Mrs. McIntyre did not represent perfection. None of us did. But she did represent integrity—something that very few people truly have when it comes to living by the creed that they preach.

She worked hard to personally embrace our principles for empowerment. And it was through her work, her presence in our school, that I was reminded of the value of P^3 Commitment, Innate Power, Personal Assets, Global Efficacy, Individual Responsibility, Sense of Self, and Shared Accountability.

Through her voice, her choices, and her dominion, I learned how to make the program better. Through her ability to come up with local solutions to what appeared to be global problems, we did make our program better.

As the author of the empowerment model, I was proud to have her in front of my students.

Through her service and the service of so many others who worked at PSGL, we taught the students how to learn. And we taught them about empowerment.

STUDENT HIGHLIGHTS

Although 90 percent of our students were impacted by conditions of poverty, service learning was the most effective in dealing with some of the more serious cases of the disenfranchisement experienced by these types of students in the learning process.

Craig and Carrie are two examples of this experience. When they first started PSGL, they were overlooked for leadership opportunities within service learning because of their disposition.

They eventually became a part of my 10 percent who were specifically assigned to serve as my student leaders. Teachers did not know how to properly respond to them because of their inclination to be either "difficult," "disrespectful," or "defiant."

But as I personally began to work with them, I learned that their disposition, which appeared to be challenging, was driven by their mistrust and lack of regard for the institution of schooling.

Their stories show how PSGL, through SBC's service learning program, restored some of their trust and reestablished their regard. By embracing these students' natural disposition to challenge, to talk, and to fight for independence, Craig and Carrie assumed operational roles that had a lasting impact on our program.

Craig

Craig's trouble was that he was extremely high-strung. He could not focus long enough to get work done, and he was incredibly mouthy.

Although I later discovered that he had an interest in global problems and a unique way to devise local solutions, he was unable to function within the autonomous structure of the GLC7 format (already discussed in chapter 2).

While Craig was considerably more active and social than his peers, he had an unprecedented way of intellectualizing social issues. He was even passionate about what he learned and his ideas for resolution. He just found very little motivation to individually manage a project.

Until I found a way to tap into Craig's motivation (because every student has a button that activates their motivation), I tapped into Craig's disposition. I found a way to use his energy level and his constant need to talk.

The first thing I did with Craig was to use him as a student speaker. When I had public speaking engagements, where I had to talk about our school's projects for global solutions, I took Craig. He was very engaging. In a dynamic, yet extremely casual format, Craig wooed the audience and established public partners for our school.

The confidence booster from this experience somehow was the motivating factor for Craig to become more serious in the GLC7 program. He actually initiated a meeting with me to negotiate a plan to make up his missing work.

We allowed Craig to make up his missing work, but in exchange, Craig was required to serve in a service learning capacity as a project lead. By coaching his peers and providing project direction, Craig worked to enhance the learning of others.

Not only did we positively impact Craig's advancement as a student, but Craig positively impacted our advancement as a school.

Carrie

I also worked with Carrie. She was initially overlooked as a student leader because of her challenging disposition.

Unlike Craig, Carrie did her work. But she also was very much a part of conflict between the girls at the school. Repeatedly, Carrie's name came up when student fights occurred, and several times, Carrie had to be detained to circumvent a classroom fight from erupting.

Carrie really was not a defiant student. But she could be "disrespectful" when questioned by adults.

Not only was I Carrie's principal, but I also had the privilege of also serving as her teacher. In this role, I learned that Carrie had a deep desire to be understood. And when she was misunderstood, she felt deeply violated. This feeling caused her to fight back, and as a result, she was perceived as "difficult" and "disrespectful."

Although I could see Carrie's emotional needs, I did not initially cater to them. Carrie had enough people attempting to make a connection with her but disappointing her instead.

Although I am now a mentor for Carrie, I chose to not approach Carrie as a mentee in those early days when she was my student.

I decided to focus on her hidden strengths. While Carrie had a mouth on her, meaning that she could easily attack someone verbally, she also had impeccable organizational skills.

For this, I activated a service learning role for her as my student administrator. In this role, she helped to track the production of my class.

Administratively, she kept the class moving by documenting students who turned in their daily work and students who did not. She was not only efficient but she was also honest. If she did not have her own work (which was rare because she knew she was now being trusted), she told the truth.

Her exemplary work immediately identified students' needs. Before the class was over, she would say, "Ms. Dye, these are the students who did not turn in their work."

I would then call the students under question over to cross-reference her work. Ninety-eight percent of the time she was correct and I was able to immediately address the problem of the missing work. Because of her, my grade book did not hold a lot of zeroes for missing assignments.

Once I established a relationship with Carrie based on mutual respect, I was then able to get closer to her personal needs. While I am not at liberty to discuss the emotional scars that she eventually shared with me, I will state that they were there.

Never trying to serve as her psychologist or her mom, I did exercise my right to serve as her teacher and principal. I related to Carrie (as with most of my students), and I knew that Carrie's trouble was not related to discipline. It was related to misunderstood need.

A year later, Carrie told me that she appreciated my approach with her and her peers. In her opinion, I was able to deal with her not as she was but as she had the potential to be.

While she is correct, I am sure that Carrie would have never grown to feel understood had we not used our service learning program as a platform for her to be understood.

Service learning never transformed Carrie to be meek and mild. But the empowerment model is not about meekness. It is about effectiveness.

Because she did not have to fight so much to be understood, she grew to use her energy, her voice, choice, and dominion, to meet her own needs. And as my student administrator, she was able to establish a different identity and reputation as a scholar.

While she earned a respect among the staff for her effectiveness, PSGL grew to earn her respect as a transforming agent.

Of course, Carrie has had other strong role models to pave the way for her. Her mom, her older sisters, her pastor, and a host of close friends continue to work with her on her empowerment and her effectiveness.

IN CLOSING . . .

Because the heart of my pedagogy is founded on social change, it is only natural that I have come to really appreciate the idea of service learning. When I was a student teacher and I had my students writing their local alderperson to address neighborhood issues affecting them, I was using service learning to teach city government.

Then when I was a teacher and I had my sociology students go into elementary schools to identify classroom norms, group think, and personality traits, I was using service learning to teach about the socialization process.

And more recently, when I redefined scholarship and integrated students into the operational processes at PSGL, I again was using service learning to teach. Through this process, students learned about leadership.

Service learning at our school was not used in the traditional way it is used in other schools. While we did go out into the community to serve, I believe the true value of the program was in how we authentically shared power with our students.

Service learning gave our students dominion. Through this dominion, they were able to use their voice, their choice, and all the other traits of empowerment.

It is here that students came to fully understand power and how it could be used to self-actualize.

FOUR

Additional Programming

The Global Leadership Curriculum 7 (GLC7) and the Leadership in Action: Self, School, and Society (LASSS) were the two essential highlights of Preparatory School for Global Leadership (PSGL) for many people. Our program received recognition for our ability to engage urban at-risk learners in a project-based learning program that was rigorous and truly student centered.

And then there were others who recognized our program for the leadership stature of our students. The way they greeted visitors in the building, the way they engaged the public with our program's highlights along with their personal stories of development, our students impressed others and represented the vision of our school to others.

It is important to note, however, that project-based learning and service learning are programs successfully used in other schools. But there are many more schools that attempt to use these two methods that have not found success.

It certainly is not because the programs do not have merit. And I really hope that the students are not used as scapegoats for a failing program. When I hear statements such as "if the students would only do their homework," "if only students were better behaved," or the classic "if only parents were involved," I cringe.

These are not the reasons why these programs do not work.

The problem lies in our inability to understand the full nature of our work as educators. As discussed in the last chapter, we tend to forget the real work of students or misunderstand it. Because they do not value what we value, or because they do not act in a way that we can identify with, we assume that there is a limited range in which we can engage students.

"Men boil at different degrees" is a slight modification of a Ralph Waldo Emerson quote. I was introduced to this quote when I worked at Marva Collins Preparatory School in Milwaukee, and it really impacted me as a teacher. I already believed that each student wanted to learn; however, this quote made me focus on the method, the technique, and the timing in which each student's desire for learning was activated.

Each student has the capacity to learn whatever is presented. My job as the educator is to find, access, and activate the approach that speaks to them.

If I drive from Wisconsin to Tennessee, the quickest route is for me to take Interstate 94 to 80 to 65 and I will get to Tennessee in approximately nine hours. But if I know that Chicago, a city that I must pass through on 94, has a major event that is causing severe traffic jams, I may decide to take 94 to 294 (the loop that avoids downtown Chicago) in order to get to the south end of 94, to then travel to 80 and then on to 65.

Yes, this route may lengthen my trip. But if my aim is to get to Tennessee, I would be willing to go the route necessary to reach my destination.

This is what good teaching is about. It is about finding an alternate route to reaching our objectives. We cannot say that students cannot learn the material because there is a traffic jam. When students are not equipped with the skills or the dispositions needed to learn the material, we must employ our own skills, our training, to get students to the desired destination.

Finding an alternate route also does not mean discarding the curriculum selected for the program. Usually, curriculum is selected because it has been thoroughly examined and appropriately explored as a resource in helping students to achieve.

This ridiculous pattern of teachers, schools, and districts to discard programs and processes to only adopt new programs and processes for the sake of student achievement grieves me. First, there is really no forward motion. If there were, we would not have the achievement rates that we have.

My grandmother always used a quote from the Bible: "There is nothing new under the sun"—meaning that it does not matter the curriculum, the methodology, or the innovative design (not even my own). What matters is a stick-to-itiveness and a resolve to find the route in which students need to learn within that curriculum.

To discard the curriculum only to start up a new one is like canceling the road trip to Tennessee because of the Chicago delays and deciding to go to Nebraska instead. Every time there is a roadblock, we do not cancel our trips just to pick new destinations. This simply keeps us stuck in stages of influx.

I said all of this just to say that project-based learning and service learning are incredibly good programs for students, even at-risk learners. There must be, however, a commitment from all the stakeholders involved to work diligently to find a way to make it work. Unfortunately, there have been times when these instructional programs have not worked in schools for reasons that have been misunderstood. As a result, those methods (or programs) were changed and/or canceled.

At PSGL, when there was turbulence or gaps in our central programming, we looked at ways to make it work. It is what we believed in. It was never about having a charter school that drove me to go after a charter contract. It was about a way of teaching and learning. When it got tough, I did not resort to changing the programming. I could not do that, as it would have violated the spirit of the school. As a result, I was forced to find ways to make our program successful.

FIVE

The Power of Direct Instruction

As I stated in chapter 1, I really appreciate Bloom's taxonomy and its framework for varying levels of cognition. This tool for teaching helps to ensure that all students are learning to the level that really promotes empowerment.

It is typically the higher-order thinking process that most educators aspire to teach. We want our students to be able to analyze, synthesize, and evaluate, as this is the stage when students and the subject matter truly merge into one. Together they take on a new life, introducing new perspectives and new ways of thinking.

When students really engage in critical thought, we as teachers, especially social studies teachers, feel validated. We feel like we are truly teaching.

Chapters 2 and 3 were about just that—higher-order thinking. Project-based learning and service learning are methods that require students to think critically. By applying, synthesizing, and evaluating, students are able to reach higher degrees of knowing, moving beyond being consumers of information to being contributors of it.

GLC7 required students to study global problems by effectively using information governed by state standards in language arts, math, science, and social studies. The effort of solving those problems as well as implementing those solutions required the higher-order skills of application, synthesis, and evaluation.

The same is true for LASSS. Having students manage and direct specific areas of responsibility required the access of higher-order thinking.

So, without a doubt, empowerment certainly requires the use of Bloom's upper-level skills.

But there is a challenge with limiting empowerment to higher-order cognition. It is especially so when educators are fixated with it. We forget that Bloom's pyramid is based on a progression of skills, grounded in the notion that one skill set is needed to promote the next.

Teachers get so consumed with promoting upper levels of cognition that they fail to develop and reinforce lower levels. As a result, students get stuck in a learning experience that is frustrating, to say the least. They are asked to synthesis reading materials that they do not really understand, and they are asked to apply knowledge when they have not really gained such knowledge.

In all honesty, promoting all levels of cognition is tough. Just like some teachers are consumed with upper levels of cognition, other teachers (especially those in urban school districts) limit their instruction to the lower levels. In those classrooms, textbook and worksheet activities drive the learning experience.

Meeting the full range of Bloom, simultaneously embracing the individual needs of learning (within the broad context of academic, emotional, and cultural diversity) and working within the restrictions of set teaching systems (such as time, standards, and tests), is not an easy task.

As a result, many people focus on one end of the spectrum or the other, rarely able to establish a pedagogy that embraces all levels of thinking and knowing. This is unfortunate, in that polarized instruction disconnects students from the learning process.

Empowerment is about connecting students to the full dimensions of learning. It is about a way of teaching (and interacting with the urban learner) that generates the power one needs to produce, prosper, and promote growth.

Schools that limit their instruction to constructivist-based programs such as GLC7 and LASSS fall short of empowerment in that they fail to recognize the critical need for basic skill development. At-risk learners, by the definition of some, are students who are at least two grade levels behind. To think that this academic delay will mend itself by turning students loose to construct learning is a fallacy.

Equally as false as this notion of students with learned helplessness providing remedial services to themselves is the notion that at-risk learners cannot work independently and constructively. It is believed by some that students who are marginalized, especially African American learners, cannot achieve with project-based and service learning.

Core Instruction was used at PSGL as the unique approach to the phenomenon of polarized instruction. Having access to the full day, we had room to provide a constructivist approach to learning, as well as providing instruction to build and reinforce basic skills and concepts.

In traditional environments, a school is founded on one learning philosophy or the other. PSGL was grounded in the belief that different modalities were needed to engage diverse learners in the full range of cognition. While GLC7 and LASSS emphasized upper levels of cognition,

Core Instruction promoted the lower levels of memorization, comprehension, and recall.

By providing instruction for basic skill acquisition, this program standardizes the approach to individualized teaching and learning and meets the unique needs associated with the urban learner within the traditional systems of time, standards, and tests.

CORE INSTRUCTION

Core Instruction is different from the philosophy embedded in the work of GLC7 and LASSS, where according to Lauren Resnick, in *Performance Puzzles: Issues in Measuring Capabilities and Certifying Accomplishments* (1994), knowledge is based on what students can produce or how they perform.

Quite the opposite is the case for Core Instruction. In this curriculum format, another philosophical strand of Resnick (1994) is at work. Here, knowledge is based on what students can recall and how they respond appropriately to stimuli.

In GLC7 and LASSS, only the environment is controlled, allowing for students to engage in a more undefined, yet higher, process of cognition (creating an authentic and genuine space for performance-based learning).

But with Core Instruction, both the environment and the process are controlled, creating a situation where students reproduce detailed knowledge for specific situations.

This type of learning constitutes the basic levels of Bloom's taxonomy, giving students the skills necessary to participate in project-based learning and service learning.

It was our belief that students could not produce quality projects if they could not perform basic functions such as reading, writing, and computing. Further, we believed that students needed to have access to a bank of core skills and concepts (readily available upon demand or need), in order to successfully walk in authority and make effective decisions.

Core Instruction was the instrument used to build this reservoir of information, equipping students with recall capacity when engaged in higher-order learning.

Besides preparing students for GLC7 and LASSS, the second objective for Core Instruction was for students to obtain "proficiency" status on districtwide tests.

As these assessments are generally grounded in isolated skills and concepts and would hardly fall into the category of being integrated, holistic, or thematic, the impetus to Core Instruction was to provide students with a framework of knowledge that was conducive to the ways in which knowledge is measured at the state and district level.

INSTRUCTIONAL PROGRAMMING

Students engaged in Core Instruction during a period called Knowledge Block, which was the second block of the day. Unlike Project Block and Service Block, which were each 90 minutes in length, Knowledge Block was 120 minutes.

Core Instruction originally focused on reading, writing, and math. However, in the later years, we began to focus more on math and science (as these areas had the greatest gaps when we looked at the results of standardized tests).

Regardless of what material was being covered, it is important to understand that Core Instruction was more about the process for learning than the content.

Remember, the goal of Core Instruction was to equip students to function successfully on projects and on district assessments. Therefore, Core Instruction was about mastery and not about exposure.

Using ability-based groupings, standards-based objectives, direct instruction (the methodology and not the curriculum), and daily and weekly tests, we were able to zero in on specific skills and content targeted for district test and project performance (as the needs were identified).

Ability-Based Groupings

Originally, Core Instruction was to be limited to specific grade levels; however, once we realized that very few students were on grade level, we created ability groups that were skill-level specific instead of grade-level specific.

Because of the small size of the school and the seven grade levels in our charge, we were only able to staff three different ability groups: primary (skill level equivalent to grades 4 and below); intermediate (equivalent to grades 5–7); and upper (equivalent to grade 8 and above).

Through the diagnostic tests that were administered at the start of each quarter, students were grouped accordingly (see chapter 6 for more information on diagnostic tests).

While it is easy to question the broad ranges of each ability group, this strategy for grouping had a positive impact on student achievement, as opposed to when students were left in groups based on their assigned grade level.

There was not one grade-level class where all the students fell within one academic range. Because of the diverse academic levels of our eighth-grade class, eighth graders tested in all three ability groups: primary, intermediate, and upper.

Students in these grades rarely tested on grade level. Instead of having the teacher differentiate each lesson for students functioning across thirteen different grade levels (K–12), we limited the range, allowing teachers to focus on only three grade levels.

The same held true for the other five classes (fifth, sixth, seventh, ninth, tenth, and eleventh).

With instruction now being directed toward a specific range and students being appropriately matched to this range, a different type of classroom environment emerged.

Students who would shy away from raising their hands or participating in class (the same students who tended to be disruptive) were suddenly engaged. Completing homework, going to the board, and volunteering to help their peers were signs that students were finally in a class where the instruction made sense.

The ability groups allowed students to feel good about learning, because content and skills were aligned to their learning levels.

We even saw an acceptance of older students being grouped with younger students. Of course, they initially did not like it; however, within a week of feeling connected to the learning process, these students opted to stay in those groups.

Typically, we bartered with students when they resisted their group placement. Through a conversation, we negotiated a trial period, and we were honest about the advantages and the disadvantages of the assigned group.

Because of this honesty, students trusted our direction and were willing to give the group a chance. When they got there, they realized it was a good match for them. It was a place where they could "feel smart."

It is important to understand, however, that students moved in and out of these groups. In a traditional tracking system, students are tested and then they are permanently placed.

Through the methodology of Core Instruction, students were tested four times a year. They understood the correlation between these tests and their assigned groups. Because of this understanding, teachers and students would strive for and celebrate upward mobility.

A true culture of scholarship and achievement emerged.

Standards-Based Objectives

Core Instruction was heavily grounded in the notion that instruction should be driven by standards-based objectives. We believed that state learning standards provided the framework for achievement and concrete objectives provided the direction for such achievement.

While textbooks were used as resources, they were not used as the guide for learning. Textbooks simply could not speak to the individual needs of our learners.

This was the role of our teachers.

So, using standards to create daily and weekly objectives, teachers made learning relevant and safe for our students. They were expected to publicly display the objectives and to verbally reinforce them throughout the lesson.

My job—or the job of my lead teacher, who later assumed the role of instructional leader for the building—was to do walk-throughs to ensure that teachers were promoting our framework for an objectives-driven, standards-based class.

Students did not understand that the walk-through process was directly related to their teachers. When we came into the rooms, students would work hard to show us they knew the learning objective.

Of course, we did not correct students' misconception of our presence in the class. When students felt the need to memorize the objectives, they also became more focused on learning. We discovered that this memorization paved the way for the lessons and added the additional clarity that was needed.

Students also started to make connections between having an objective and learning. As a result, they began to look for them as critical elements of the instructional environment.

Once, when a fairly new teacher was struggling with classroom management, one student accused the teacher of not having an instructional focus. She said, "If you do not give us an objective, how do you expect us to know where we are going?"

Although I know this made the teacher uncomfortable, the teacher later admitted that from that moment forward, she vowed to never get caught again without an instructional objective.

Ironically, this disposition of students to look for class objectives increased students' understanding and appreciation for state standards.

Through GLC7, students had to use state standards to justify rigor in their projects. By examining the standards-based objectives in Core Instruction, students strengthened their understanding of how to break a standard apart to extract concrete objectives.

The need for both students and teachers to work with standards-based objectives created a partnership for learning. On occasion, you would hear students and their teachers engage in an intellectual conversation (and sometimes a debate) about the appropriateness of the standard or the accuracy of the objective.

The bottom line is that standards-based objectives promoted scholarship among our learners, and it ultimately allowed our learners to feel and act like scholars.

Direct Instruction

The method of direct instruction was the required instructional format for Core Instruction. Whereas teachers served as facilitators for project-based learning and supervisors for service learning, Core Instruction had teachers serving as directors.

Using a lesson format of five specific stages, teachers directed students through a clear, concrete, and predictable platform for learning.

While teachers initially felt stripped of their autonomy and creativity because of this rigid format, they quickly saw the psychological value for learners.

By submitting to a daily set structure, a routine was established that allowed students to partner in the learning process. Teachers did not have to spend time transitioning students from one phase of the lesson to the next. Instead, students knew the transitions, worked with the teacher to make these transitions, and held their peers accountable if transitions were disrupted.

When we as teachers creatively develop and implement lessons, we can unfortunately cause confusion. In our creativity, students lose a sense of safety and lose out on an intimate knowledge of the lesson. This lack of certainty about the learning environment causes students to feel uneasy, as they do not know what to expect.

To use a road trip analogy to make my point, let us talk about a trip from Atlanta to Charlotte. The first few times I took the trip, until I got comfortable with the drive, I had to focus on where I was going. I had to look at the time, look at the signs, and I had a heightened sense of caution to prepare myself for the unexpected.

Because I was not familiar with the trip, little bends in the roads, splits, and lane merges were a big deal.

But after taking that trip many times over, I did not need to focus so much on the signs. I could expect the splits and the lane endings. Ironically, the scenic value of the trip, the same scene that had been there all along, got my attention because my attention was no longer processing the direction of the trip. I could simply drive and enjoy the ride.

This experience is identical to what students experience in the classroom. In order to function and to be successful, students have to pay attention to the simplest things. Instead of really throwing themselves into the intrinsic value of the lesson, they are concerned with technical details such as timing, changes, and shifts, and they subconsciously have to be on guard for the unknowns—the unexpected.

With Core Instruction, students can predict the timing sequence, the shifts, and they can feel safe in their ability to anticipate the unexpected.

Instead of spending time fretting over the unexpected and managing the anxiety that arises with not knowing, they can better direct their emotional energy toward learning.

Once the teachers mastered the format of our approach to direct instruction, our classrooms were orderly, learners were highly engaged, and students who typically opted to fail were now choosing to learn and pass.

Daily Quizzes and Weekly Tests

At the end of every class, students were quizzed on the daily objective. The quizzes were anywhere between three to five questions long and extremely concrete. They did not require analysis. They simply required basic answers.

Each day, students anticipated this quiz (again, because the format was predictable), and they looked forward to demonstrating their mastery (especially since it did not require a lot of time or emotional energy).

Teachers used the results from these quizzes to understand how to move forward with the lesson the following day. They also used the data from the quizzes to determine how to modify homework assignments in preparation for the weekly tests.

Every Thursday we tested for Core Instruction learning. As we mentioned in chapter 3, Thursday was how we defined the end of the week, as Friday had a different function.

If it was Thanksgiving week, when students only attended school on Monday, Tuesday, and Wednesday, then Wednesday was how we defined the end of the week. And it was Wednesday that students were tested on the weekly objectives.

Regardless if we tested on Thursday, on Wednesday, or even on Tuesday, every week there was a test. And every week, the tests were based on weekly objectives.

We had a specific way of monitoring the integrity of weekly tests. By examining weekly lessons plans, we measured the tests against the daily objectives. We wanted to make sure that there was an alignment between what was being taught and what was being tested.

Tests were supposed to give students the opportunity to demonstrate mastery—not to give teachers a reason for teaching.

Everyone knew that these tests were functional, in that they produced data that was used to tell stories about students' learning needs and then used to make decisions about our program on a day-to-day basis.

Like quizzes and like objectives, tests were concrete and predictable. We respected the emotional energy surrounding tests; therefore, they followed a specific format to eliminate surprises for students and to give them a sense of understanding and peace about what to expect.

Because we tested every week, we did not need to overtest students. Tests were not lengthy, they were not tricky, and they were not confusing. They were approximately twenty questions in length, as it was the aim to specifically focus on the learning goal for that week.

EMPOWERMENT CONNECTION

Core Instruction directly connects with three out of the seven empowerment principles: Personal Assets, P³ Commitment, and Shared Accountability.

Personal Assets

Core Instruction does not really tap into the External Resources or the Interpersonal Resources of Personal Assets (typically reinforced in GLC7 and LASSS). However, it does specifically focus on the intrapersonal resources, allowing students to build a reservoir of information to be quickly accessed in order to tackle the higher-order thinking that is required in school and in life.

P³ Commitment

Because students are expected to master learning on a daily and weekly basis, the P³ Commitment does come into play. A driving theme of Core Instruction is mastery and performance, which easily translates into producing results on weekly tests (and daily quizzes).

It is amazing to see at-risk students embracing this weekly testing experience, especially when they have shied away from it in the past.

Students want to show mastery. They want to be scholarly. The ability-based groups,and predictable format of Core Instruction give them the opportunity to prove it.

Shared Accountability

While it was not really mentioned as a part of the instructional programming for Core Instruction, the Friday schedule did allow for the principle of Shared Accountability to be activated.

As already stated, Friday was a day of special programming. For Core Instruction, it was a day for instructional reinforcement.

When students did not pass the weekly test on Thursday (or the second-to-the-last day of the week), a special class was designed on Friday (or the last day of the week) for the lesson to be retaught and for students to retake the test.

Reteaching and retesting is an example of Shared Accountability in that all players are held responsible for student mastery of the skills and concepts for the week. The teacher is held accountable for teaching the objectives in a way that students can learn, and the students are held accountable for studying and demonstrating that they have learned.

TEACHER SHOUT-OUT

Most of the teachers highlighted in this book were valuable to our school because they were able to function in different roles. Such was the case with Ms. Smith.

Over her three years of service with our students, Ms. Smith functioned in the capacity of a Project Block teacher, a Knowledge Block teacher, an advisor, and an operations manager.

The reality is that titles and roles were not so significant at our school—at least not so much in the earlier years. If there was a job to be done, Ms. Smith did not get caught up in her job title. If she was there when there was a need, then she was also there to meet the need.

"Whatever you need me to do" were words that I frequently heard from Ms. Smith. When she joined our team, she came truly willing to be a team player.

Not only was Ms. Smith a team player, she was also very loyal. She was extremely committed to the vision of our school and worked hard to ensure that others also maintained the integrity of our mission.

I am sure Ms. Smith could tell her own story as to her level of loyalty to our program, but in her absence (yet with her consent), I will say that her years of experience before coming to PSGL validated the need for our program. She would repeatedly say that the structure provided at our school was a much-needed fixture to be added in other urban classrooms.

Because of Ms. Smith's experience teaching in the urban classroom, she came to the table with a set of skills that others had to be trained for when hired as PSGL teachers. True, there was a learning curve for Ms. Smith, and there was a training process in which Ms. Smith worked with other staff to learn the instructional mandates of our program. But she also brought a fundamental quality to the table.

Ms. Smith did not have to be trained on the value of order and structure. Quite the contrary! Ms. Smith took dominion in the control and order of her classrooms. Unlike other staff members, we did not have to teach this philosophy.

There were some who accused Ms. Smith of wanting to have too much control; however, I never identified her challenges to be an issue of too much control. Instead, I believe Ms. Smith had to learn how to incorporate students into the management process so that they could share the responsibilities associated with order.

You see, it is easier to teach about shared management to an individual who values control and order than it is to teach about shared management to an individual who champions student freedoms and limited controls.

While we were an empowerment-based school, we did not believe individual empowerment guarantees individual freedoms. Freedom is never free. It always comes with a price. Someone always pays.

PSGL respected this principle and did not leave the doors open for interpretation as it related to the rights of individuals. We created environments where the definition of empowerment was clear, the rights of the whole were prioritized, and individual freedom, while respected, was monitored.

This value system was at the heart of Ms. Smith's pedagogy. While it may have appeared to some that she wanted control, those of us who championed empowerment knew she was simply trying to have order. And Ms. Smith welcomed our training as we worked with her on a shared experience of power and control.

Unfortunately, there were teachers who wanted to promote a feel-good, let's-all-hold-hands-and-sing-together-in-harmony classroom experience, yet created an environment that housed every type of personal offense imaginable.

In the absence of control is chaos. And in chaos, one's personal well-being is definitely sacrificed.

Understanding the adverse affects of such chaos on student achievement, Ms. Smith, in her passion for structure, worked collaboratively with others, helping them to embrace this belief.

Ms. Smith was ideal for Core Instruction because she embraced the instructional mandates of the program down to her core (where it was not about doing her job, it was about doing what she believed in).

She respected the aim of excellence and mastery.

Maybe it was the influence of her dad, whose military experience accepted nothing short of excellence. Or maybe it was her own position as a parent that gave personal relevance to her work. She wanted her own children to achieve and assumed that other parents wanted the same.

And her commitment to mastery definitely had an impact on our students. When we aligned Core Instruction with ability-based grouping, it was Ms. Smith's group that consistently changed.

She definitely influenced upward mobility. Students were intent on testing upward into her group, and once there, they were challenged by her to move upward out of her group.

Ms. Smith was assigned to the intermediate group, where students were testing in math at a grade level of 5, 6, or 7. By the end of every quarter, these students consistently tested out of her class (testing at grade level 8 or beyond).

The last quality that made Ms. Smith an ideal teacher for Core Instruction was her ability to relate culturally to the students. She had an exceptional ability to take math concepts from the state standards and create math activities that connected to the personal experiences of our students.

Textbooks cannot do this. Textbooks can have a multicultural section, but they cannot equip teachers with the ability to teach the concepts in the students' language.

While Ms. Smith was regarded as being "mean" by some of the students, the majority of the students appreciated her math class. Because it was in this class that learning made sense. The skills and concepts that sounded so foreign to students in the past were now familiar, and students found themselves enjoying math.

This experience eventually made its way to students in the lower group. Ninth graders who tested at the fourth-grade level were placed in the primary group (the K–4 group) and worked really hard to test out of that group just so they could test into Ms. Smith's intermediate group.

I found out later that Ms. Smith really promoted the quarterly tests as achievement indicators for her students and for her own performance.

I think Ms. Smith did good things for students at PSGL, especially in Knowledge Block where she was committed to Core Instruction. Because of her desire for structure, mastery, and cultural relevance, Core Instruction was a match for Ms. Smith. And she was definitely a match for us.

Thank you, Ms. Smith.

STUDENT HIGHLIGHTS

By the time we implemented the full nature of Core Instruction (especially with the ability grouping and retesting on Fridays), we saw consistent improvement with our students' core academic skills.

While all students showed progress in at least one area of testing, the greatest impact of our program was seen with students who had significant delays.

To illustrate my point, let me share with you the experience of four of our unique learners. Two of the students were diagnosed as having a learning disability, and the other two could have easily been diagnosed as having an emotional disability.

All four of these students were fifteen years old at the time of testing; none of them were in their regular grade and none of them were testing on grade level.

But every last one of these students showed grade level-gains after being at our school for at least a year. While I am sure that GLC7 and LASSS had a significant impact on the total scholarship of each student, it was Core Instruction that we believed caused the academic growth that is measured by standardized test.

Because of the age of these students, placing them into the primary group was not easy. As was to be expected, these students did not want to stand out and did not want to be viewed as being academically delayed.

Through the coaching of our staff and their creative use of service learning to activate students in nonacademic roles, these four students eventually embraced their groups and found themselves experiencing significant growth.

Student 1, who initially tested at the pre-primer level (classification for a nonreader), was put in the primary group (it was the lowest group we had available, as we did not have an ability group specifically for nonreaders). By his last year of testing at school, he had gone from being a nonreader to a reader (testing roughly between the first and second grade).

Student 2 initially tested at the second-grade level; she was also placed in the primary group. By the end, she had moved to the intermediate group (because she was testing at fifth grade).

Students 3 and 4 were in the eighth grade, although they both should have been in the ninth, and they were both testing at the fourth- and fifth-grade level. Both of these students were with us for only one year, but they still made two-year gains in either reading or math.

I wish I could identify these students by name, as they truly need special recognition. But with the sensitive nature of their stories, I thought it would be better to focus more on their accomplishments than their identity.

IN CLOSING . . .

Core Instruction is probably a program that could be used in isolation. It definitely has a stand-alone quality. But, I would never feel comfortable using Core Instruction as the primary learning method in a school.

While it provides for the development of basic skills, the skills assessed on standardized tests, I simply do not believe this program alone fully empowers students.

Students need to be able to think critically. They need to be able to analyze. They need to be able to function in the higher aspects of the learning pyramid outlined by Bloom.

While Core Instruction could be modified to address higher-order thinking skills and incorporate more group work instead of the single use of individual seat work, it would never be able to compete against GLC7 or LASSS (which is totally committed to higher-order learning).

The best way to use Core Instruction is in conjunction with other programs that promote holistic learning (such as project-based learning and service learning). Usually, these programs cannot promote mastery of basic skills, just as Core Instruction cannot promote the development of leadership skills.

As educators, we have to define and embrace our philosophy of knowledge. And with that, we have to find the instructional method that will tap into this knowledge base for our students.

At PSGL, we believed that knowledge is in what you know, is in what you are able to do, and is in what you are able to become. Only through the use of Core Instruction along with GLC7 and LASSS, could we embrace all dimensions of knowing. As a result, we were able to strategically address all levels of Bloom's taxonomy.

SIX

Assessments

With all there is out there on student achievement and how to measure that achievement, it is a wonder that more schools have not integrated an assessment course to position students as partners in the testing requirements mandated by state agencies.

We can create partnerships between the school and parents, between the school and the community, and even between the school and staff; however, what happens when you establish a partnership between the school and students?

The theory of cognitivism—teaching students by teaching them how we teach and how they learn—gives great strength to incorporating students as partners in the whole quest to improve student achievement.

And in a world where achievement is primarily based on standardized tests, I think it is only fair to incorporate a model that trains students on standardized testing and involves them in a preparation process that is both effective and holistic—effective in that it meets its objective in getting students to perform at their highest potential on those tests, holistic in that the test training is not really limited to a lesson, a workshop, or even a class.

Instead, the training taps into the total child. Psychologically, spiritually, emotionally and intellectually, the student understands the role of the test and becomes fully present and engaged in the training process.

It is important to note that I do not think standardized testing is the sole determinant of academic achievement status.

While I can understand the argument (and this is only in part) that standardized tests measure basic skills in core academic areas, I do not believe these tests can measure other skills essential for successful living, such as collaboration, communication, problem solving, analysis, and the use of resources and technology.

How do you standardize these skills and still allow for the creative interpretation of the learner?

In making a case for holistic development and achievement, I want to be careful to not position myself as being averse to standardized test scores because I am not. I think they have a value and a role.

But I also know that there are other factors, more of a political nature, that will cause us to omit experiences that students need in their development, if we are not careful when making critical decisions on curriculum and methodology.

I think we all can agree on the developmental needs of students, but I think we fail to understand the cultural and political context of these needs and therefore pretend that all students are running the same race, starting at the same starting line, and have the same end zone as their target.

This is not the case, and this is the fundamental weakness with limiting a school, a teacher, and a student's progress based on the data derived from standardized scores.

At PSGL, our work had a twofold objective. First and foremost, our mission was empowerment, so we had to make sure our curriculum and our assessments spoke to our achievement in this area.

But we also had a contract to provide public education. And the context of our contract put certain mandates in place requiring our students to achieve at specific levels on standardized tests.

For me, there was no other way to do this but to involve students as partners. I can fuss all day long about the political nature of testing but, as I like to say, "It is what it is." I was comfortable with the testing requirements, as I knew they were only one aspect of our program. We were so much more than a test score. So, for this reason, I did not resent them.

There was another reason why I was comfortable with embracing the mandate of district-level testing. While not qualitative, the quantitative process did provide some data necessary in our work for empowerment. When we work with students on achievement and goal setting, numbers generated from these tests are great resources.

So for me, the challenge was not the test but creating an environment where all forms of assessing could be incorporated, valued, and achieved. Hence came the creation of Institute as an orientation class.

Originally, Institute was designed to teach students about their own psychosocial nature. Through this class, we wanted to empower students to maximize on the resources available in life so that they can self-actualize—so that they can produce, prosper, and promote growth. Believing that our program, our charter school, was one resource out of many that were available to them, we were going to teach them how to use our school to get them to a place of greatness.

But as I began the work of the school and I looked at the broken condition in which students entered our program, I knew that if we did not incorporate testing and assessments as a key orientation theme, students were never going to shift in their attitude toward testing. As a result, they were never going to make the kind of progress for which political stakeholders look.

So orientation for our program also included orientation for testing. By teaching students about the political and cultural nature of testing, schooling, and even teaching, we created a partnership for achievement.

INSTITUTE

Institute was a one-hour course offered as a way of training students on the central themes and operations of the program. While orientation in nature, it was not limited to new or incoming students. Instead, it was used throughout the students' tenure at the school to keep them connected to the whys of what we do along with the hows.

To provide focus to the curriculum, students learned about various assessments of the program, what they measured, and the significance of the data extracted from these assessments. At the same time, students learned techniques to enhance their performance on such assessments.

Objective 1: Portfolio Assessment

Each year, students developed and presented a leadership portfolio. The portfolio had five sections that highlighted students' growth in the areas of leadership and empowerment. In January, they were required to submit a draft of the five portfolio sections, and in June, they presented the final work.

The presentation section of the assessment was made to a panel of assessors consisting of teachers, parents, peers, and community partners. The first part of the presentation was to submit the portfolio to the school one week prior to their scheduled presentation. This submission allowed teachers to verify portfolio completion and to prepare and support the student in the remaining areas of the assessment.

The second part of the assessment was for students to make a fifteen-minute presentation on their portfolio, outlining their growth and ultimately advocating for a specific grade.

The third part of the assessment did not include the student presenter. The student was required to leave the room and allow time for the assessors (including student assessors) to deliberate. Once all assessors agreed on a grade for each section and also a final grade, the student presenter would come back into the room for the final part of the assessment.

The last section of the portfolio required students to engage in a dialogue regarding any questions that arose in the deliberation. Ultimately, the dialogue was to provide for discourse just in case assessors did not grant students the grade originally requested. Students would at this time reinforce areas in their portfolio that were underrepresented or misrepresented during the second part of the assessment.

In the end, all players—assessors and the student—had to agree on the final grade.

Institute prepared students for this assessment by providing them with a context for each section of the portfolio, as well as providing them with sufficient time to complete the work.

Institute also taught students how to effectively communicate throughout the four stages of the process, as well as allowing students to practice presenting and giving their peers constructive feedback.

Finally, Institute taught each student how to use the learning experiences at the school to provide meaningful artifacts for this assessment. Students learned how Project Block, Knowledge Block, and Service Block (along with Institute and Advisory) provided for leadership and empowerment, and they learned how the work they produced could be pulled together to create a powerful portfolio.

Objective 2: Quarterly Diagnostic Assessments

Every quarter, students were given a reading, writing, and math assessment to determine value-added growth for each quarter. This assessment was important, as many of our students were far from being on grade level. Here is where we were able to show growth in our program, even if a student did not meet "proficiency" on the annual district-level test.

Using the Jerry Johns to measure growth in reading, the Terra Nova to measure growth in language and math, and student writing samples to measure growth in writing, teachers facilitated a multi-tier diagnostic evaluation to collect and synthesize data on students' progress.

Institute was used to teach students the value of diagnostic assessments and the value of various program components at PSGL, as relating to the assessment (specifically Knowledge Block).

Objective 3: The Annual State Assessment

The state (through the district) annually used the Wisconsin Knowledge Concept Exam (WKCE) to measure student proficiency in reading, writing, and math. Every year, all students participated in this assessment, while students in grades eight and ten had to participate in additional tests related to science and social studies.

As with the quarterly assessments, Institute prepared students for the WKCE. We provided them an overview of the different sections of the

WKCE, along with equipping them with test-taking strategies so as to lessen the anxieties associated with taking the test.

Objective 4: Daily Behavior Assessment

Every day, teachers and staff administered a daily behavior assessment that recorded positive and negative behaviors of each student. Institute was used to create a shared definition of "negative" and "positive" behaviors and to provide a platform for students to contribute to this assessment in a proactive and productive way.

The daily behavior assessment had an accountability value in Advisory (see chapter 7) that required students not only to be held accountable for their behavior but to also reflect on their behavior and set goals for improvement.

Institute taught students how to reflect and to control their behaviors by equipping them with thinking and reflecting tools. Edward de Bono's six thinking hats, as well as his acronyms for thought, were taught to students so that they knew how to assess an abstract situation for its personal and social value.

Objective 5: Knowledge Block, Project Block, and Service Block Performance Data

In Institute, students learned about production and performance in each instructional period and the curriculum used for each. They learned strategies on how to improve their daily and weekly performance, as well as the interrelationships among learning programs and assessments.

Objective 6: Quarterly Scorecard

Every quarter, all data collected from each instructional block as well as quarterly and annual assessments and daily attendance and discipline data was organized into a quarterly scorecard to create a leadership profile for each student. Through Institute, students learned the five tracks of the scorecard, they were kept current on their profile status, and they set goals to push themselves forward in their own progress.

INSTRUCTIONAL PROGRAMMING

Institute was primarily offered as a one-hour workshop within Service Block or Project Block. Additional time for Institute was allocated within our special Friday programming to allow for ongoing portfolio development. During testing season, however, the schedule was typically modified to give more time to Institute, thereby ultimately increasing the time available for test preparation.

Because of the dynamic nature of Institute, all teachers and staff had a role in the course. First, all teachers had to promote the central theme of empowerment (the concept and the program), as well as participating in successful assessment preparation.

Traditionally, however, the lead teacher, the advisors, or I (in the earlier years) would lead in formal Institute instruction.

In a high school model, Institute can be used to earn credits in psychology and sociology, as the premise of the five objectives requires students to learn about the psychosocial nature of learning and schooling.

EMPOWERMENT CONNECTION

Because Institute is an orientation for the program and the program's assessments, all seven of the empowerment principles are activated as themes through this curriculum. However, there are several principles that have a more intentional relationship with the program: P^3 Commitment, Sense of Self, and Shared Accountability.

P^3 Commitment

Because students are learning how to be successful within the program and they are also learning how to use the program to be successful outside of school, Institute has a direct relationship with the principle of P^3 Commitment.

While P^3 Commitment is implied in other areas, Institute consciously promotes the concepts of self-actualization. This goal of self-actualizing, of producing, prospering, and promoting growth, is the overriding mission of all five SBC learning formats.

When students enter the program, they are required to submit a baseline portfolio that demonstrats their commitment to production, prosperity, and promotional growth.

We do not require portfolios to be fully developed and sophisticated (like the final one presented at the end of the school year). Instead, we are looking for students to demonstrate awareness of our mission and verify that their enrollment is about the promotion of this mission.

Sense of Self

The principle of Sense of Self deals with the five lenses with which we see ourselves. Within the daily behavior assessment of Institute, students learn these five lenses, not just in theory or as concepts, but in application.

They take a look at who they are as it relates to the function of the school and their relationship with peers, and they find ways to establish spaces and boundaries to protect self and protect others, all while promoting the mission of the school.

Shared Accountability

Because of the assessments channeled through Institute, students faced the outcomes of their choices and behaviors on a daily basis. Regardless of the level of the outcome, their behavior was translated into raw scores. Institute engaged students in a process that analyzed this data and therefore, allowed students to own the results — their leadership profile.

TEACHER SHOUT-OUT

Because Mrs. Vertal had become one of the pillars of the school, it was easy to place her in Institute.

Being an Institute teacher required that you know the program inside and out. You had to understand the theoretical framework of the school. You had to understand the methods employed. You had to understand the students in their current state and in their potential state (by way of empowerment training). And you had to believe in the idea of production, prosperity, and promotional growth.

There was no other person besides Mrs. Vertal who could have stood by my side as my partner in empowerment.

She and I would often joke about being spiritually connected, because there were many times when there were no words to guide us in our work of urban empowerment, yet we stood together intuitively understanding each other's motives and intentions.

The story of how I got to know Mrs. Vertal is quite dear to me. It was one of the first warm days of May, and I had decided to sit outside to review résumés for positions I had recently posted. I was new at the whole résumé-reviewing process and therefore took extra time really scrutinizing profiles and waiting for them to speak to me.

Ironically, Mrs. Vertal's did. Sometimes I would go back to her résumé to really see what it was that made me give her résumé a special marking. On the surface, I thought it was her use of terms such as "constructivism," "collaboration," and "hands-on learning," but when I reflected on it later, I saw that there were other candidates who used these words as well.

Mrs. Vertal would often laugh about it because she said these were simply the concepts she learned in college. She thought she was supposed to use them to apply for a job.

But on a deeper level, I truly think it was divine for Mrs. Vertal to come and work with me in my mission for empowerment. First, she got lost and did not show up for the interview (she had never been to the city). And when we rescheduled the interview, she almost turned around once she got to the area of the school. Not only had she never driven into the city, but she had never before seen the "ghetto."

Mrs. Vertal impressed all of the students when she did her mock lesson, and she impressed the interview panel that consisted of potential parents and community and board members.

But it was not until Mrs. Vertal wrote a teacher reflection, months after she had been hired, that I knew the universe had sent her. In her reflection she talked about the sadness of the students' self-identity. When she had students complete a project on their perception of greatness, the portraits of the individuals portrayed as great were people who looked like Mrs. Vertal. They were white.

Mrs. Vertal talked about how she would have felt as a parent if one of her kids had come home with a personal portrait of greatness and the cultural representation of the person was skewed.

This is not to say that students cannot promote diversity in their views of greatness. Please do not misinterpret this point.

The message for Mrs. Vertal was that students did not associate greatness with being brown. When she questioned the students on it, the discussion only reinforced her fears. Our students had very low self-images, and Mrs. Vertal believed the students needed not only the academics, but they also needed a program that would build their spirit and strengthen their personal identity.

Mrs. Vertal was relentless. There was nothing in our program that she could not learn. She had an extremely committed work ethic and was very loyal to the mission. By the time Year 5 rolled around, Mrs. Vertal could teach Institute, as she had personally lived each of the program's five areas.

Serving as a Project Block teacher, a Knowledge Block teacher, and a Service Block teacher and performing the duties of an advisor and program manager, Mrs. Vertal knew the ins and outs of each curricular program. Not only did she understand them in a technical sense, but she also understood the spiritual value of each. She taught in those blocks as if empowerment was her personal mission, not like it was just a job.

As a result, she was very instrumental in showcasing the work of urban empowerment for other nonurban staff members I hired.

Diversity has always been important to me personally and professionally. However, when I walked into the role of school leadership, I realized how difficult it was to bring people of various backgrounds together to serve one singular mission.

The point I want to make in this chapter, while discussing Mrs. Vertal, is that she emulated urban empowerment from a nonurban perspective. I could not do that. I am urban — very urban.

Together, Mrs. Vertal and I taught Institute at different times, offering different perspectives within the same mission. Like me, she knew how to extrapolate and disseminate student data in a way that they could manipulate and arrive at certain conclusions. To tell students a story is one thing. But to allow students to analyze data for themselves and come up with the same story on their own—that is another thing entirely.

I trusted Mrs. Vertal with the mission of urban empowerment and believed that through her, the work will continue in ways I would never be able to promote.

STUDENT HIGHLIGHTS

Lisa was the one student who was classified as being the student principal. Having an extreme capacity for depth and insight, Lisa embodied the program as if she was one with it.

If there was ever a student I had conflict with teachers over, it would be Lisa. While Lisa showed me the side of her that was thoughtful, mature, and empowered, she showed an entirely different side with others.

It was not that I disregarded the difficult side of Lisa that she presented to other teachers. I just wanted to push them to see the fullness of Lisa, more than what showed. If they could, I fully believed that she would be the strongest asset for them in the classroom.

Like the other teachers, I had an initial connection with Lisa that was not all warm and fuzzy. Because we both had big personalities, there was an unspoken war as to whose personality would prevail.

What Lisa did not understand is that I enjoy the unspoken challenge presented by students. While on the outside a student is trying to present himself or herself as being tough, bad, and heartless, I see something quite the opposite. I see fear, need, and a desire to be recognized.

When most people meet Lisa, they do not see this side of her. And as much as I have worked with her on her presentation, she still refuses to show people just how vulnerable and needy she is.

Instead, she puts on one heck of an act to let other people know that she can and will hurt them before they can hurt her.

My introduction to Lisa was when the school first opened in 2004. It was actually the very first day of school, and all the students were waiting outside to come in. There were other staff members outside, and typical to most teacher-student relations, students were not being held to a standard that would be acceptable for them to enter the building.

So I went outside to promote the standard that I wanted. I refused to wait to get all the students inside before going over my list of rules. Instead, I demonstrated my expectations in deed before I presented them in creed—meaning that I walked the walk before I talked it.

All of the students responded to my presence. They settled, got in a straight line, and stood up tall and straight.

But for Lisa, the students' reaction to me was like a challenge. She wanted me to know that she did not jump for anyone. She took a step back, put her hands on her hips, and looked at me from toe to head (not head to toe). Anyone from the urban community knows the meaning of this nonverbal gesture. She had just presented me with a challenge.

Don't get me wrong. I am all for student empowerment, but I do not play when it comes to respect. Because I am going to hold myself accountable to respecting my students (even when it is difficult), I expect them to do the same. And I accept nothing less than that.

I am a warrior in that I play to win—every time. But I am also strategic. Very much so. Because of this, I was very comfortable in losing the battle Lisa had presented, just so I could later win the war.

There are two mistakes that teachers make in this area of warring with students. First, they misunderstand the war, and therefore, they move in to win a battle. They fight the wrong cause, and as a result, they are never able to position those students on their side when the battle is over.

Then there are those teachers who put off the battle for the sake of the war and never return to win the battle *or* the war. Nothing makes you lose the respect of students faster than when you let them walk over you.

I do have a point here. As I have said, there are times when you must lose the battle to win the war. You let the student think that he or she has won by allowing him or her to win the immediate (in-your-face) challenge. But you must, without a doubt, come back and win the war (which is respect, accountability, and growth). Otherwise, your whole credibility is lost.

And for the sake of this book and the ultimate message that I want to send out about student empowerment, urban education can be a battle. For anyone who thinks otherwise, they are delusional. Students do not need us to be weak. They need us to be strong. And above all, they need us to be fair.

So when we fight thought patterns of failure, behaviors that impede progress, and attitudes that block achievement, we must do it to win. But we must be fair with our approach. We must win the war without losing the student.

So that was the situation that existed between Lisa and me that early September morning. But I know students even when they are difficult. I know that ultimately they just want someone they can trust and respect.

I did not push Lisa to get in line. As a matter of fact, I ignored her, walked right past her as if she did not exist. In my mind, I was letting her have her way of not getting in the line the way I wanted, but I had every intention of letting her know my standards and my commitment to have those standards honored. It just did not have to happen right in that moment in front of the other students and staff.

I actually ignored Lisa that entire day. Well, I ignored her through eye contact. But I felt her. She was taking me in. I was the head authority, and she was calculating in her mind what the school was going to be about and what she was going to get away with.

And while she made these assessments, I went throughout the day and I told my story. I let her know, indirectly, that I come from the same place that she comes from. I have the same needs that she has. And I have the same fire in me that she has to get what I want.

In my stories, Lisa saw someone she could identify with. This was my intention. I allowed my intuition to pick up on her story, and I went through my database of personal experiences and told those I figured she could relate to. And I was successful. Because at the end of the day, Lisa walked up to me and apologized for not starting off on the right foot with me. She said, "I think I am going to like this school."

My response? I told her that I believed I was going to like having her in my school—but tomorrow when I came out for my line, I expected her to set an example.

She did. From that moment forward, Lisa became my ally. She was not perfect, as she gave teachers a run for their money. But I never asked her to be perfect. I asked her to grow and to learn. That was my priority, and she embraced it as hers.

It was easy for me to wrestle with teachers over Lisa. While she was tough in their classes, they eventually witnessed a different side to Lisa when she interacted with me. This display of her dual nature gave me a platform to teach my staff about her needs and the needs of our most difficult students.

I highlight Lisa in the Institute section because Institute encompassed the entire program. And like Mrs. Vertal, Lisa knew it. She knew the techniques. She knew the philosophy. And because she was tough, popular, and very strong willed, she became someone who could promote the program in its operations and influence the achievement of others.

Through our relationship and her leadership, I was privileged to have a group of student leaders who worked hard to promote empowerment.

Institute did not have the bells and whistles for students to shine. It was a place where they, along with Lisa, could recharge.

IN CLOSING . . .

The approach of incorporating assessment and achievement data into the teaching process has been with me for a long time. I am sure some elements of cognitivism were there from day one, but I can recall distinct strategies of this method starting in my fourth year as a practitioner.

I was working at Grand Avenue High School as a social studies teacher (teaching government, geography, and U.S. history). I was struggling with getting my students to turn in their homework. They participated in their class activities but were really disconnected from the daily homework assignments I was giving out.

At the time, each of the four teachers on my team had a fifty-two-inch television in the room to be used as an instructional aid. With the help of our school's technology teacher, I hooked the television up to my Mac computer. I then created a spreadsheet, on which I assigned each student a confidential number and then listed all of their assignments for the class. I also entered a formula that showed students' averages on any given day of the quarter (based on the up-to-date data entered into the system). When students walked into the room, they could see the assignments that were turned in, the assignments that were missing, and the current status of their final grade.

For some reason, this data impacted the students. First, they rushed to get to class on time because it was during the class start-up that they could walk freely to the television to get their data. Second, they tried to negotiate a way to fill the spaces for missing assignments, understanding (in concept only) that these zeroes lowered their average.

Finally, the students began to turn in assignments on time so they could receive full credit (as opposed to the partial credit they received when they turned in work late). All of a sudden, the assignment board had value. They wanted to pay extra attention when I closed out the class and reviewed the assignments that would be due the following day.

Now, simply having the digital gradebook on display is not the full nature of cognitivism. However, I integrated gradebook management as part of the class process, and therefore it became a part of our learning experience.

We learned how to manage our work and our learning spaces. We learned how to average grades. And we learned how to effectively problem solve challenges between our personal and school lives that interfered with homework completion.

From this activity, students learned how to be successful in my class. And when they learned how to be a successful student, they also learned the material that I was teaching. Win-win.

Taking the extra step to incorporate this system in my class strengthened my students' role as students, helped me get students to complete my assignments, and ultimately caused students to learn the subject matter that I was responsible for teaching.

When we teach students fundamentally about themselves and we teach them how we are teaching, we share the power of knowledge. Instead of teachers keeping this important information of how to teach and learn to ourselves and placing ourselves in the end-all position of causing academic growth, we should share it.

By doing so, we show students we respect their capacity to understand and that we trust that with this knowledge they will join us in the mission for academic achievement.

We empower students any time we share power. Whether power is innate or power is in one's ability to manipulate resources to solve problems, teachers are remiss if they omit students from the gift (and responsibility) of power.

At PSGL, we taught students how to learn. We empowered them.

SEVEN

Accountability

When looking specifically at accountability, an emotional vibration is sent out the moment it is activated.

On both sides of the table, if you are an adult who is fighting for the well-being of a child, and even if you are a child who is fighting for the well-being of your own identity, there is an emotional challenge that cannot be denied.

There are a number of reasons why real accountability is difficult (even in the cases where outcomes to actions are positive).

First, and foremost, accountability is personal. And many times, it is associated with likability.

Accountability has a personal nature to it, especially when it centers on sanctions. The individual being held accountable or those emotionally connected to the process feel as though sanctions are being applied because the individual is not liked or is not popular.

This is especially true for teenagers. The passion behind the words "You are picking on me" or "That's not fair" speaks to the spirit of likability. Although in most cases this interpretation by the child is illogical, in the mind of the one being held accountable, associations are made to the degree in which he or she is liked.

The second reason why accountability is difficult, which is very much connected to the first, is that when applied, there is not a clear division between accountability and punishment.

Accountability should be about teaching. But when you have the wrong people in the position to hold others accountable, accountability is not really about that at all. Instead, it is about a right-back-at-you and a stick-it-to-you disposition that is used for getting even.

I do not care how well the act is supported with data. If accountability has an emotional quality, a sting at any level, it is punishment. When we do not check in with our emotional state while we are holding students accountable, it is easy for our actions to come across as punitive. And for this reason, students have an adverse reaction to being held accountable.

Now, once we are sure that students are not being punished, we still have one more area of emotional difficulty to contend with.

Admittedly, accountability impacts and even restricts power. Sometimes, outcomes to our actions can cause unwelcome changes in our environment; when this happens, it is a natural response for us to use our innate power (our voice, our choice, and our dominion) to reverse those changes.

And when we cannot (because of some type of accountability sanction limiting the function of innate power), this, my dear friend, is the other place where accountability becomes emotionally challenging.

At PSGL, these emotional challenges were very much a demanding part of our practice, but we did not shy away from them. We did our best to deal with them, as accountability was the only way we could ensure an authentic program for empowerment.

P³ ADVISORY

P³ Advisory was a course that placed students at the heart of a program that was designed just for them. It was our way of ensuring their commitment to empowerment.

For any program that is about serving people, you have to find a way of putting those very same people at the center. They must be able to serve themselves.

Empowerment is not about saving others. It is about giving individuals the power to save themselves. Everyone must be committed to this belief, as without it, empowerment does not exist.

The Objective

To be accountable is to be subject and liable to your actions. Because our program was about empowering students in very real ways, accountability was a very real part of our program. Students had to face their choices and take ownership for them.

If students could have real power and responsibilities, then they also could have real accountability. To not hold students accountable for their actions, in my opinion, is an insult to their power. If there are no outcomes to their assigned positions, then there is no authenticity to those positions.

In service learning, students had real power. We did not employ a student council program in which students were activated as leaders within a specific segment of the week or a portion of the day.

Instead, we had an empowerment program where students were activated as leaders the entire day. All day and every day, students could and were expected to use their voice, choice, and dominion to manage and make decisions like other players within the school (staff, parents, and partners).

When students acted in ways or made decisions that promoted the mission of empowerment, the behavior was acknowledged and celebrated for the related outcomes.

Likewise, when students acted in ways or made decisions that hindered the mission of empowerment or had an adverse impact on the program, the behavior was acknowledged and addressed. Either way, students faced their actions, their dispositions, and their responsibilities toward leadership.

This was how our school approached accountability. Good or bad, right or wrong, justifiable or inexcusable, students were subject to their role as leaders, recognized for their strengths, and liable for misappropriated decisions.

INSTRUCTIONAL PROGRAMMING

Through instructional focus, reflection, discipline, and goal setting, students were connected to their choices and their actions in ways that were not only reactive but also proactive. They faced themselves intrinsically and holistically, resulting in an accountability process that promoted the end result of production, prosperity, and promotional growth.

Instructional Focus

Before, after, and during school, Advisory incorporated a method called instructional focus. This was how we emphasized leadership objectives with students and their behaviors during traditional and nontraditional periods.

Using the daily behavior assessment method (discussed in chapter 6), students were graded on how well they used nonstructured time as a place for practice. As a result, lunch and the commute before and after school became a part of the Advisory program, thereby reinforcing the theory of connected schooling.

The second method used for instructional focus was silent reading. Whether this was a group reading (choral reading was allowed during silent reading time) or individual reading, after lunch, students were expected to read with the purpose of learning about the work and lives of other empowered individuals.

Through works of fiction or nonfiction, students extracted leadership lessons and principles valuable for personal application.

Proverbs

Each week, a schoolwide proverb was selected to give thought to students' behaviors. Through the message of these proverbs, students were able to see themselves in a way that was almost spiritual.

I have always been amazed at how proverbial quotes or sayings impacted students.

Years before I became a school director, I used proverbs as a part of a Black history project. For each day of February, a significant quote by a well-known African American would be selected and displayed in the classroom. Students would then reflect on its meaning and identify ways in which the quote impacted them.

Students looked forward to class each day to see which quote was being presented. They even began writing their own quotes, and ultimately the activity extended beyond the month and became a part of our practice.

Then when I went to work at Marva Collins Preparatory School in Milwaukee, I was reintroduced to proverbs. It was there that I saw the schoolwide value of proverbs as they became words of wisdom for instruction, for behavior management, and for school leadership. Not only did students respond well to the quotes, but so did staff.

There probably was no greater impact on me than those quotes. They made me reflect on my practice as an educator but also on my assignment with empowerment. Through these quotes, I started hearing my call into school leadership. While I was not excited about the idea of becoming a school administrator, these quotes made me face the real notion that my work in education extended beyond the classroom.

Seeing the effectiveness of proverbs in other school environments naturally made me incorporate them into the SBC model. And there was no better place for the proverbs than the P^3 Advisory program.

In Advisory, students were held accountable for their behavior and choices throughout the day (as discussed in chapter 6). Just as the proverbs held me accountable for fulfilling my professional mission when I was at Marva Collins, students at PSGL also faced their life's purpose with these messages and had to account for their daily development toward this end.

Using proverbial empowerment as part of a schoolwide method was not as easy as simply picking quotes to be used by everyone in the school. We learned quickly that not all proverbs were for the advancement and empowerment of students and not all teachers were able to differentiate between effective proverbs and ineffective ones.

We found that proverbial empowerment could be a challenge for teachers and staff. Just because a quote had great literary value did not mean it would inspire student growth. Quite the contrary! Some proverbs had an adverse affect on students, making them feel belittled and hopeless.

This challenge was fairly easy to address. First, I limited the selection of the schoolwide proverbs to key staff and key student leaders.

Then we implemented additional training for staff, teaching them how to use proverbs in a mission-driven environment. We taught teachers how to incorporate the proverbs into instruction and how to continuously connect students to the vision of empowerment.

Finally—and ultimately this is the point of our program and certainly solidifies our use of proverbs—students were empowered to address the misuse of proverbs. Frankly, they knew how proverbs were to be used. Whether students selected them or not, they had to meet the approval of key student leaders.

We allowed students to have voice in this area because it meant that students were personally internalizing these quotes, and they even looked forward to using them when they were being held accountable.

Reflections

Each night in Advisory, students were asked to reflect on their day of learning. They had to identify the objectives for each subject, they had to differentiate between what was mastered and what concepts needed further reinforcement, and they had to acknowledge their level of productivity in our project-based learning program.

These reflections held students accountable for learning. Students knew that each day before leaving they were going to account for their production, their prosperity, and their promotion of growth. It became a daily practice to account for their presence in our empowerment-based program.

As a side note, this process also had an impact on behavior. The more you can engage students in their academics, the less time and energy they have for disruptions.

In addition, this reflection process also gave room for students to express an area of concern. Often, we would find out problems that were weighing heavily on them and impeding their ability to learn, causing them to be more agitated and easily manipulated into emotional conflict with a staff or peer.

Of course, reflections were a proactive approach to discipline. Because we did not misappropriate the value of the reflection process by using it as a replacement for discipline, we acknowledged its worth on the front end of working with students and maximized it for all that we could.

Discipline

When students' behavior mounted to the level of chronic disruptions or safety violations, discipline measures were enacted. Again, behavior was monitored by a daily behavior assessment, and students understood the line of demarcation between minor disruptions and chronic disruptions.

Ninety percent of the time, students could anticipate disciplinary actions. Because discipline was about accountability and not about punishment, there was a high level of predictability between behaviors and outcomes. Our system for discipline allowed students to manage their choices, because the end result was very predictable.

Now, it was not as easy as simply making rules and enforcing them — not with an empowered student population. The challenge was in the predictable nature of the program. Students knew at what point discipline would be enacted, and many times, they would play the game right up to the edge.

If twelve minor behavior disruptions generated "chronic disruption" status and ultimately activated a suspension, some students would interpret this as a free pass for them to be disruptive eleven times. And even though the disruptions were minor, eleven of them can be quite challenging for a teacher.

But in the grand scheme of things, eleven minor disruptions are better than one major safety issue. Even more so, eleven minor disruptions are better than twenty. And for those of us who have worked with difficult populations, redirection counts for a highly independent, energetic, or misdirected child can easily exceed twenty in a day.

I am by no means suggesting that we tolerated each student to be disruptive eleven times a day.

Our discipline process had several legs to it that allowed us to combat those clever students who knew how to work the system. As a result, students who activated the chronic disruptive behavior status at the twelfth offense were not doing it to be intentional. There usually was something else happening in the classroom.

For the most part, our clear and consistent approach to discipline was a deterrent to manipulating the system.

The first leg of our approach to discipline was to activate an "Extended Advisory." In short, this is what you and I would remember from our school days as a detention. However, we did not call it detention, as the aim of Extended Advisory was not in providing a punishment.

Honestly, we found out early in the game that many students enjoyed being kept after school. Here is where they got more adult attention and more one-on-one interaction. So we did not rely on the "punishment" of keeping them after school to deter student disruptions.

Extended Advisory was a way we took students through an instructional process that had them connect with their actions, learn how their behavior was toxic to our learning environment, and commit to making better behavior choices the following day.

We incorporated several methods into this extended period to get students to meet the objectives of Extended Advisory. The first thing we did was to have them complete an additional reflection. Using the daily behavior assessment that was generated as part of the Institute component of the SBC curriculum, students could clearly see a list of offenses identified by the staff (for that day only). Students had to address the offense in each class by stating what happened, why it happened, and what should have happened.

They also had to find a way to synthesize the proverb and the empowerment message of the proverb into this reflection. They had to clearly show a deep understanding of the proverb through a discussion on how their behavior did or did not support the proverb's message.

Through this additional reflection, specifically on behavior, teachers were able to discover root issues and address them. If a student was documented for talking in class when he or she had simply asked a peer a question about an assignment, this reflection process would allow the two of them (student and teacher) to come together and resolve the confusion.

If a student felt frustrated in how the teacher was treating him or her, they could discuss the details in this reflection process and initiate a discussion where the teacher could learn different ways of interacting with that particular student.

The reflection process was not always taken seriously by students or by staff. But through the continuous work of leadership training for students and for staff, they eventually caught the value of the process and became loyal to it.

The second leg to discipline was our use of community and relationship. For the most part, our students appreciated the closeness they had with staff. They did not want to violate it. The teacher could use his or her relationship with students to curb the number of offenses in his or her classroom. In addition, the teacher could use his closeness with key students to influence other students (new or more challenging) that the teacher was not close to.

The idea of student relationship (not student friendship) goes a long way. As a school leader, this is what I worked hard at modeling the most. When teachers have positive and healthy relationships with their students—I don't care what type of student it is—they don't have a lot of discipline problems.

Many teachers try to incorporate student relationship into their practice but are unsuccessful. I witnessed this on two levels. As a colleague/peer, and as an administrator/instructor, I saw how teachers misunderstood the needs of students, especially at-risk students, and use friendship as a substitute for relationship.

But friendship is not the answer. I would always tell students, "I am not your friend. I am better than a friend." Friendships require reciprocity. And while there is a reciprocal value between students and teachers, the relationship should not be based on a mutually beneficial interaction. I am going to promote the good in my students even when I do not like what they do or what they stand for.

My students typically have no problems with my telling them how I feel because at the end the day, they can trust me to be fully committed to their needs. Whether I like you or not, I respect you. I want what is best for you. I want to empower you. And this, the mission of empowerment, is and should always be the basis of student relations (not likability or friendship).

The third leg to discipline was student-teacher negotiations. Students and teachers would barter with their power. If a student wanted to activate a teacher's power to drop a suspension, the teacher would then activate the student's power to make better the choices the next day.

This negotiation system was not minor or loosely managed. It was well documented and tracked. When students (or staff) failed to honor their end of the bargain, the problem was then elevated to a higher authority. Neither the teacher nor the student really wanted that, so for the most part these negotiations were honored.

Negotiations as relating to discipline were monitored. We had to ensure that students were being accountable and could not use their persuasive and charismatic personality to influence teachers to violate our system.

When all players were fully engaged in their duties and responsibilities, these negotiations were quite effective. First, they made students feel powerful as they activated their voice, choice, and dominion. Second, these negotiations strengthened student-staff relations, building on the premise of trust and even loyalty that must exist in order for student achievement to occur in a classroom.

The fourth and final leg to discipline was our tracking, intervention, and expulsion process (supported by data from the scorecard tracking system discussed in chapter 6).

At level 4 (in a 1–6 system), the student's seat in our program was threatened. Students did not get expelled until they reached level 6; therefore levels 3–5 activated special interventions to restore the student back to good standing (levels 1 and 2).

We were very clear on our model. While we enrolled any student interested in the program, his or her placement was kept by upholding the commitment to empowerment (demonstrated by achievement data that placed the student at levels 1 and 2).

In five years, we only expelled one student who had reached level 6 of our tracking system, and we successfully "coached out" four students who had reached level 5.

As a staff, we really worked hard with those students who teetered on levels 3 and 4, doing our best to get them out of the red and into the functioning place of level 2.

At level 3, an individual plan was activated through the input of the advisor and the individual student. Usually, students at level 3 were distracted by other priorities in their lives. The level 3 work of the student (see goal-setting section below) positioned the student to reclaim leadership status by helping him or her focus on the goals of empowerment.

A student who could not redirect his or her behavior (with the help of his or her advisor) eventually moved into level 4. At level 4, all stakeholders for the student were activated: the student, along with his or her advisor and teachers, the school leader (either myself or my lead teacher), and the parent.

Every person participated in the intervention plan, where the goal was to help the child return to good standing and uphold the leadership standards established.

For the most part, this team-based approach to student intervention was successful. But there were times when a student moved from level 4 to level 5. Because we already had an intervention in place at level 4, we modified the plan at level 5, assuming that something was wrong with our original insights.

When a student had to move to level 5, this usually meant that there were deeper problems that were not discovered at levels 3 and 4. Maybe there was a school issue (staff training or instructional programming), maybe there was a parental issue (working more hours and having less time at home to monitor the child), and maybe there was a personal issue with the student (such as depression, drugs, or abuse).

It was easy to mask the real problems at level 4 because at that level, standard intervention methods were employed. They usually did not get at the root of severe academic or personal problems.

But when a student reached level 5, we talked honestly about what was tried at level 4 and what issues prevailed. Because we were a small, close-knit community, a level 5 intervention meeting really was effective at tapping into the heart of the problem—the undisclosed crisis.

Once we were able to be honest about this crisis, all parties were able to find more effective ways to participate in a solution.

Because of the honesty that led to real solutions, students typically did not stay on level 5 for very long. It may have taken a minute to get students to a level 2 (which was the desired level), but they typically moved off level 5 quickly.

In those rare cases where students did not make progress and were progressively heading toward a level 6, we activated another teamwide meeting and began having conversations about placement.

In those discussions, we explored the likelihood that our program was not an ideal match for the student. It was then, before going to the expulsion process of a level 6, that we found another school for the student to attend.

Goal Setting and Coaching

Every quarter, students' scorecards were updated and published for them and their families. As a school, we reviewed the data on these scorecards and coached students through a goal-setting process.

We used the data of the scorecard as well as the detailed data of the daily behavior assessments to set goals. Goal setting was personal, as only students, not their teachers, could examine themselves and make commitments that they could live up to.

The advisors, however, would internalize the goal of each student and work with him or her to meet the goals.

Only advisors (and the lead teacher and I) could serve as coaches. To effectively coach and not get caught up in friendship building required a special disposition and training.

The staff at PSGL had to respect this policy.

ADDITIONAL LEADERSHIP

While accountability was primarily employed through Advisory, the work of accountability had to penetrate the entire community. The reality was that there was more work to the implementation of accountability than simply holding students accountable.

Accountability was not limited to Advisory. Frankly, it had to exist as a major theme of empowerment. Right there with student power, accountability was a key pillar to our program. Because of this, it required the involvement of all school players.

Just as we trained students, we also had to train staff and parents. We had to be strategic with our training, as working with adults is significantly different (yet surprisingly similar at the behavioral level) to working with children.

Students, regardless of how difficult they are, typically are more open and trusting than their teachers or their parents (generally speaking).

Therefore, training the adults also meant working through personal barriers that had nothing to do with PSGL but everything to do with their individual construct of schooling, authority, accountability, and need for personal validation.

When we look at things on the surface and fail to recognize and even appreciate these core challenges at the root level, we cannot be effective.

We truly tried to address these root issues in our training. While it was difficult, we incorporated a training process that allowed adults to bring their personal issues to the table so that we could ultimately learn how to partner for the sake of empowerment.

Staff Training

Training staff was huge. For the most part, teachers need students to respect them more for personal validation than for instructional value. As a result, teachers hold students accountable as a way of protecting their person. But accountability cannot be personal. When it is personal, it is based on emotions. When it is based on emotions, accountability turns into punishment.

One way we circumvented the personal and emotional mistakes of discipline was by incorporating my personal mantra of "firm, flat, and fair." This was the energy that we entered into accountability decisions, sanctions, and negations.

In our efforts to train students on depersonalizing accountability, we had to make sure that it actually was not personal. This training required a lot of time, energy, and money, but we did it. Staff embraced it and were willing to learn it; therefore, we found a way to train them for it.

Staff training was not only used for teaching the method of firm, flat, and fair communication, it was also used to train staff on what not to do. As I said before, only select personnel could coach students, and it was difficult getting new teachers to follow this policy.

Typically, new teachers wanted to coach students because they thought this was a method to get students to like them. But coaching can only be effective when students respect you. Coaching does not build respect. Coaching is *built on* respect.

Truly, we only wanted new teachers to document for the daily behavior assessment process (which then equips the school to hold students accountable). Goal setting could only occur when there is ample data to work with (which is why documenting behaviors was critical).

The other problem with allowing untrained teachers to coach students is that they did not have the resources to coach effectively.

When we coached students, we often had to take them through a process to build a case for them to see the value of our suggestions. And we had to negotiate and barter with students in order for them to try to implement our suggestions.

A teacher had to be trained on the processes of building a case for coaching, and they had to be given access to additional power and authority in order to activate intervention strategies outside of the established systems used by the school. New teachers did not have this power.

So, while we had to train students on the accountability aspect of empowerment, we definitely had to work with staff. With students, it was a matter of teaching them the connection between empowerment and accountability; for teachers, it was about teaching them the connection, teaching them the systems, teaching them the value of following the systems, and then teaching them the systems again.

Parental Training

Additional training was not limited to staff. We also had to train parents. They too needed to know how accountability worked in our program. Just like with students and staff, where training consisted of detraining and retraining, parents needed the same amount of attention and support.

The work with parents was that we actually wanted them to serve as coaches. However, due to parents' own childhood experiences with schooling, parents instead served as champions.

When students questioned the fairness of employed consequences to their actions, we wanted parents to support us in our work with empowerment. We wanted parents to teach the child how to handle the problem on his or her own. Instead of coming to school to fight the battle for the student, we wanted the parent to teach the child the proper ways to challenge authority and to negotiate to get results.

Of course, in those cases when the problem was bigger than the student (which honestly was rare, but unfortunately this is an issue with perception—which leads to a different discussion), we wanted those parents to contact the lead teacher and partner with her to resolve the problem. And at the same time, we still wanted parents to find ways to promote the practice of student empowerment.

The flip side of parents as champions instead of parents as coaches is the case of the crowd-pleasing parent. These were the parents who would emphatically convey that they would nip the problem in the bud.

The problem with the crowd-pleasing parent is that this display of disciplinary involvement is for show because discipline is short-lived. Yes, there usually is some type of immediate discipline that follows the proclamations of these parents that the matter will "without a doubt" be resolved.

But difficult students are not usually difficult because they have not been disciplined. They are usually difficult because they have not been seen. They have not been understood. They have not been present enough in the minds of people whose attention they crave.

I know because I was that child. It did not matter the number of spankings or punishments I received. The best form of corrective action for me was to engage in an intellectual discussion so that I too, through my voice, choice, and dominion, could see the error of my ways.

I am not against a parent who errs on the side of control in order to properly raise a young person living in an urban environment. To me, it is better to have too much control than not enough when trying to navigate your child through very real and present dangers of teenage pregnancy, drugs, gangs, crime, and even police brutality.

The way I always heard it from my mother and her mother, parents would rather be tough on their child than allow life to be tough on them. When life gets a hold on you in ways that are rough, it is not easy to get from its clutches.

I tread lightly on this subject because I know parenting is hard. So in my opinion, any parent, crowd-pleasing or not, as long as he or she is trying to promote healthy growth in the child, is an asset to empowerment.

But I do want to emphasize my point that different parenting styles impacted our empowerment program in different ways, and therefore, we made it an absolute priority to engage parents in the training process.

In the end, the work we did with parents and teachers worked because we did have a well-managed climate. We had one of the highest poverty levels for our age group in the city, and we dealt with all the behaviors associated with this level.

Regardless of the behaviors that came into our school, our accountability system, our students, staff, and parents were able to work together to create an overall tone of scholarship and leadership.

All the work we put into the programming and training aspects of accountability was well worth it.

EMPOWERMENT CONNECTIONS

The Advisory program relates to all seven themes in that it works to hold students accountable for the entire empowerment process. While all SBC programs encompass the seven principles at one point or another, P^3 Advisory is unique in that it intentionally promotes six (close to GLC7, which intentionally promotes all seven): P^3 Commitment, Personal Assets, Innate Power, Individual Responsibility, Sense of Self, and Shared Accountability.

P^3 Commitment

The whole premise to accountability is to hold students to their commitment to production, prosperity, and promotional growth. How students fulfill this commitment is highlighted as part of the accountability program.

When students produce, prosper, and promote growth, they account for it, and generally their achievement is acknowledged and celebrated. When there is a breach in the three Ps, then students must answer to it and find ways to rectify the problem.

Personal Assets

While Advisory indirectly relates to all aspects of Personal Assets (internal, external, and interpersonal), it has the strongest connection with the third trait, interpersonal resources.

Three skills of interpersonal resources, collaboration, analysis, and valuing, are all activated in the Advisory program. Students are required to work with their advisors and other teachers to account for their behavior and to negotiate outcomes.

When students hit twelve offenses throughout the day, they are able to collaborate with their advisor as to the best outcome or sanction that would generate a meaningful lesson and restore their status back to good standing.

Likewise, students must also analyze their behavior. With the behavior assessment, all we do is list the offenses. We do not really know why the offenses occurred. Students through their analysis must come to this conclusion.

It is also important to note that students are part of the process of establishing the coding system that identifies certain behaviors as toxic. So when there is a breach, typically the students, through their own analysis, are able to both identify the problem and diagnose why it occurred.

Finally, when students have to interpret the weekly proverb and apply it to their person in a way that will redirect their behavior, they are activating their skills for valuing.

Innate Power

I always get excited when talking about the Innate Power of students. Such is the case as I prepare to write about how students' Innate Powers are activated in the Advisory program.

When we talk about Innate Power, we have to totally change our paradigm of what should be when relating to students. We give power to students to have control over their own person, and we bestow a level of respect to support their decisions.

This is very difficult when students make decisions that are contrary to their short-term development. As wise adults, we can see how students' decisions can have a detrimental impact at the immediate level. But if we really want students to make a meaningful connection on how their voice, their choice, and their dominion affects their person, then we must step back and allow the lesson to unfold.

Simply put, we must sit back and allow them to make poor choices so that they can feel the real sting of their decisions and ultimately learn to make better ones.

I am not suggesting by any means that we should allow students to make poor choices that will have a lasting impact on their person. I am only advocating that we allow short-term pain for long-term growth.

Such is the case with Advisory. There were times when a student would activate the need for a suspension because it was his or her choice to do so. Just because we allowed students to negotiate out of suspensions did not mean that this negotiation was required.

If a student did not want to negotiate out, we would allow them to take the suspension. We would respect their right to choose and to have dominion over their person.

True, there were some cases where students would actually manipulate the system to get suspended. Because of our consistency and the predictability that surfaced, students could work the system to get out of school.

This ability to work the system gave some students power that was quite frustrating at times. But our goal was empowerment, trumping power over punishment, allowing students to manipulate this annoying yet necessary quirk in our system.

The ironic thing about this power that we gave students is that typically they did not use it to get suspended.

Once we gave students permission to use their Innate Power (the freedom to choose the suspension), they actually chose to come up with alternatives to the suspension. It truly was quite fun at times to watch students use their power to stay in school!

Individual Responsibility

Because of the P³ Commitment, students were responsible for demonstrating a certain behavior. While they understood this concept in theory, I think they got frustrated by how consistent we were in holding them to this standard.

We made our mission and our commitment to this mission clear when they enrolled in the school, but I do not think students understood the full degree of our creed. Yes, they understood the concept. But the consistent application of our words caught students off guard.

Students understand that adults make declarations and promises that they cannot fulfill. They understand good intentions; yet they also understand the challenges of follow-through when life gets in the way.

I could not tell you the number of times students told me that they disregarded the rules of their parents or other adults. For them, the rules were short-lived. They knew the intentions behind the policy but they also knew that the policy would not be reinforced over a long period of time.

For the most part, they waited. They waited for a weakened resolve in policy enforcement, and they waited until that adult's attention was drawn elsewhere.

It was quite the norm for new students to get upset at our school. They typically did not have a problem with the rules until they were consistently reinforced.

Carrie, the student leader I talked about in chapter 3, once said, "Ms. Dye, sometimes we do not want to be leaders. Sometimes we just want to be students."

I always think of this statement. While she said it in frustration, there was so much value in those words. From her honest admission, I knew that it was not the rules that made her a leader. It was our consistency in enforcing them that reinforced her leadership.

Quite frequently, I would pull together and facilitate a Circle of Concern with my key student leaders. (Please remember, these students were typically the most challenging students in the building, so getting their voice was ultimately getting the voice of the entire student body.) Other students looked up to them. They had a lot of influence.

In this circle, I gave students a choice. They could maintain their power so as to continue the work of leadership, or we could adjust their power so they could function simply as students.

Just as staff could not turn empowerment on and off, neither could students. We were not going to allow students to say, "I do not feel like being empowered right now." So they had to choose—one way or another.

Now, we did allow some students to negotiate through the dynamic challenges associated with power and responsibility. But we did not make schoolwide changes, as that would have ultimately weakened our mission for empowerment.

So, instead of deactivating empowerment for the whole school, staff would move in to adjust the level of power and authority that individual students had.

However, once they reached a shared agreement on what was mutually beneficial for the student and the program, the agreement was binding.

Most times, students chose to wrestle with the additional responsibilities. Ultimately, they liked having the position of power, so they grew to be OK with the associated levels of responsibility.

Sense of Self

If any principle were to be highlighted as the primary principle for Advisory, then I would say it would be the principle of Sense of Self.

With Sense of Self, students had to learn how to see themselves and to position themselves appropriately in the world. Because they were held accountable to their choices, Advisory made students take a closer looker at their person. If students wanted to avoid making the same mistakes, they had to learn the motivating factor for those mistakes. They had to understand them in order to resolve them.

Students learned a lot about themselves in Advisory. While Institute taught them the theory of Debono's Six Thinking Hats, Advisory taught them the application. Through Advisory, where they had to face their actions, they used their intimate understanding of their personal hats and how they affected their interactions with other students.

Sebastian would often say, "I know that I am being a red hat right now, but I do not care." You see, a red hat is an emotional thinker, someone who does not carefully weigh the facts but makes decisions based on a feeling.

So even though Sebastian often acted with a red hat, his ability to identify this emotional state allowed him to make better choices. He would put himself on a time-out. He would tell us that he could not talk while he was he was wearing a red hat. And many times, Sebastian would come back to his teachers and peers and apologize for things he did when he was in a red hat space.

For anyone who has worked with an emotionally charged student, you know that these self-monitoring traits were quite helpful.

Shared Accountability

Because of our format with Advisory, accountability was viewed as a shared initiative. Staff alone did not hold students accountable. Students also held themselves accountable.

Because our system was predictable, students had the power of knowledge, knowing how to enter into the process as a partner and how to work together with the staff to assign an outcome.

Because the physical structure of the school was so open, it was easy for students to be a part of every action and system. For example, when there were gaps in the staff's performance, students could see it. Through our Circles of Concern and our student negotiation notes, students addressed performance gaps in the spirit of protecting and promoting the program.

Teachers were trained to facilitate this process of accountability, and they were supported when the work of shared accountability became emotionally challenging. Even though students had a right to protect the program (pointing out missing objectives or the misuse of instructional methods), they did not have a right to be disrespectful.

As with any new skill, though, students did fumble with their power and the skills to effectively use their power. But when they fumbled and were disrespectful, we enacted our systems for accountability. Here they had to account for their behavior, while at the same time learn how to better handle the situation.

TEACHER SHOUT-OUT

The teacher I want to give recognition to in this section is Ms. Guice. Ms. Guice was the right teacher to work with Advisory. She was not perfect, but she was ideal.

Ms. Guice had a way of holding students accountable while at the same time conveying her love and respect for them. It was rare that students would get upset with her when she had to enact some type of discipline. Why? Because of her ability to be firm, flat, and fair, students did not mislabel her sanctions as punishment. It was business.

We would sometimes laugh about the concept of "firm, flat, and fair," as initially Ms. Guice would enter into what I would call "mama mode." She would react, instead of positioning herself to be proactive when students did wrong.

The mama-mode trait was easy to address, mainly because in this mode, she was still trying to hold students accountable (never trying to be their friend). The problem was that her system for accountability was an emotional one instead of a technical one.

But Ms. Guice came to us with an existing framework for empowerment. While it was not exactly in the way we defined empowerment (through the seven principles), it was more than any other teacher had ever brought to our school.

So it did not take much work to teach her about the "firm, flat, and fair" approach. She was open to any method that would allow her to empower students (not play with them).

Ms. Guice was also able to transfer her gentle, yet firm approach with students over to parents. She sold the empowerment program to them in a way that I had never seen. Somehow she spoke their language. She was didactic in that way. She spoke in a way that students and parents could both understand.

Because of this, she bridged a lot of gaps for the school. We had the highest level of parent satisfaction when she was employed with us. She was a gem for promoting our philosophy, our projects, and our methods.

Thank you, Ms. Guice. We could not have touched the number of families that we did without you.

STUDENT HIGHLIGHTS

Deidra was great with accountability. All students learned the skill of being accountable for their growth and production, but a few students like Deidra served as exemplars of this behavior.

Like most of our students, Deidra had a temper on her. But she learned how to embrace the principles of empowerment to work through many of her differences with others.

It was commonplace for us to hear Deidra tell someone, "We can agree to disagree" or "I don't agree with you, but I do understand where you are coming from."

Deidra learned how to negotiate through conflict. And she employed this method when it was to her benefit.

If I explained to you her home life, you would not believe that this little girl could approach a situation so diplomatically. I do not want to misrepresent her, as she was not perfect. None of us were. But she embraced the skills for empowerment, and she was not afraid to use them with her family and peers.

Once when I went to do a home visit, I had the opportunity to speak with her mom. I am not sure what we were talking about, but her mom stopped me mid-sentence. She asked me where I was from, and I told her I grew up in the neighborhood.

She did not believe me and actually challenged me. I told her, "No, I actually grew up a few blocks from here."

She went on to say that she was surprised because, in her opinion, my speech did not signify that I had spent time in the "hood."

Deidra jumped in to say, "No, Mommy" (Pause: I think this is cute because she and her sisters really did call their mother "Mommy"—but back to what I was saying . . .), "No, Mommy. Ms. Dye just knows how to go from the street-house to the White House."

This was a phrase that we began to use at the school to teach students about differentiating their speech. Street-house is the language we used when we are in a private or an informal setting. White House language is the language we use when we are trying to impress others as if we were the president of the United States.

I was taken aback that she would take this school-related principle and use it to make a point to her mother. I think Deidra really learned to internalize the different spaces of being as promoted by the principle of Sense of Self.

She had a hunger for many of the principles that we taught. She could not always apply them because in her world, they were not always the most effective tools for survival. But I knew they were in her, as she would showcase them in times when she did not even know someone was looking.

IN CLOSING . . .

For every school that prides itself on being mission driven and then employs a separate behavior management program, disconnected from the central learning themes, I am saddened.

While I believe in my program and believe in our methods for student empowerment, I also believe there are other programs, while different, that are equally powerful.

And when I see the vision of schools lie dormant in a vision statement or in training manuals, my heart goes out. I understand the fundamental piece of accountability that is missing. I am troubled that a good program has been crippled.

If you want to see results, you must hold people responsible for delivering these results.

This is why accountability in our program was big. We could not do the work of empowerment without students (and their families). As a result, accountability was one of the pillars to our program. Right up there with power, so sits accountability.

And while there is a challenge in creating and running a program that promotes empowerment and at the same time relying on people (teachers, parents, vendors, and authorizers) who do not fully agree with the methodology of empowerment, it was a dance that I had to learn.

There is a lesson to be learned from the dynamics of this polarizing response to our empowerment program. From those people who loved giving students power yet disliked holding them accountable, and those who liked holding students accountable but did not like giving them power, I have come to appreciate the value of balance.

Empowerment that is balanced is the only real way that true empowerment can exist.

EIGHT

The Politics of Empowerment

The purpose of writing this chapter is to shed light on the many challenges of providing an empowerment-based program for urban students. While there is no single entity that will serve as the "bad guy," in this section I will reveal the barriers that made my work with empowerment more of a fight than the opportunity it was intended to be.

My overall aim for this book is to inspire a movement of student empowerment in urban communities across the nation. However, I do not want to be misleading by limiting the discussion to the philosophical and instructional elements of empowerment.

My work with student empowerment, in the practice of giving students power so they can produce, prosper, and promote growth, required me to contend with aspects that went beyond instruction and even beyond administration.

Empowerment is more than a curriculum. And it is more than a system of schools. It is a way of thinking that, when enacted, challenges the status quo and causes friction in how we interact with various players of our society.

For any teacher, politician, or even student who is intrigued with the idea of empowerment, "Empowerment starts here" can only happen when you can play with the players who are positioned to both promote and prohibit empowerment.

It is this "playing with the players" that I officially call the politics of empowerment.

Make no mistake about it. My work with the school took me way beyond my comfort zone of being a teacher leader and even beyond my growing comfort with being a business executive.

I had stumbled into a place where I had to truly be a social change agent and contend with all the forces (hidden and not-so-hidden) that have oppressed a community of people. There were times when I felt that I had become the physical representation of that conflict, bringing the battle to me in an up-close-and-personal kind of way.

Through this unanticipated role, I learned how to play with the players. Not initially but through my maturity, I learned how to deal with the politics of empowerment.

BATTLE 1: PARADIGMS AND SOCIAL CONSTRUCTS

Paradigms and social constructs are abstract realities in our day-to-day living. However real, the abstract nature of these entities can easily lead us into believing that they do not exist or that they are not real. So instead of being able to address them head-on, we tend to spend our energies qualifying them or campaigning for others to acknowledge their existence.

A paradigm is a pattern that exists within our thought process, and a social construct is a pattern that exists within social structures/interactions. Both of these are so ingrained in us that we are foolishly tricked into assigning to them a universal value.

I think we are all guilty of this—even those of us who support free thought and work hard to be independent thinkers. We have to embrace the fact that it is easy for us to hold our values and our beliefs to be right, while viewing anything that opposes those views as wrong.

This gets tricky, however. It is an egocentric notion that is misidentified as right versus wrong, truths versus misconceptions, just because it has a historical, religious, or popular foundation.

This discussion is not to debate if a universal truth exists or not. I simply want to point out the conflict or the battle that surfaces when two opposing views meet and one of those views has a fundamental yet unspoken notion of truth.

As a social scientist, the concept of dealing with opposing views is what I enjoy processing. But when these opposing views serve as barriers to forward motion and they are not verbalized or even identified, then the work shifts and a battle emerges.

It is not even a matter of debating the issue. It is about identifying it, outlining it if you will, and making visible the invisible.

And when people think their views are universal truths, especially when they have traditionally had access to power, then it is no longer about a difference of opinion. It is about maintaining the status quo, the very thing that works against the concept of student empowerment. It is this that makes me fight.

I learned how to fight the battle of paradigms and social constructs that worked against my mission for urban empowerment by first calling the situation for what it was.

I referred to them as invisible giants.

The next thing I did was make it my business to get a highlighter, finding some way of making my enemy come out of his hiding place, stand, and be accounted for. Only then could I confront it.

And usually, when I was successful at turning the invisible into a visible entity, I was also successful at addressing it. One way or the other, the giant fell, and it was me who knocked it over.

And in those rare occasions when I could not make visible the invisible or knock over the giant, I let wisdom direct me around the matter. In my discernment, there are times when I am silenced—as I believe all battles are not mine to fight.

While I like to consider myself a warrior, I do not believe in spending my time fighting battles that do not belong to me. Because in winning some battles, I can ultimately jeopardize losing the war.

The Paradigm and Social Construct of Schooling

Many of the unspoken battles that I dealt with centered on the notion of teaching and learning.

While unspoken, it was one of the easier battles, mainly because there is a network of educators out there fighting the same battle with me. I was able to draw ammunition from this network and integrate the game plan into my own building.

For example, many teachers and parents measured schooling by the traditional elements that were used when they were in school. Elements such as textbooks, school buildings, and "the principal's office" were very much a part of their reality.

So when PSGL chose to drive instruction with state standards (instead of textbooks), chose to renovate a church rectory for the instructional environment (instead of housing the school in a traditional school building), and refused to let the principal's office be a place for student discipline and time-outs, some people were upset.

In their minds, PSGL was lacking the infrastructure to qualify as being a "real" school.

I did not spend a lot of time fighting this battle. Through school choice, Milwaukee was saturated with innovative schools that were also creative in their design and format for learning.

When parents had concerns with our format, I acknowledged the options that were available to them within the city, and I celebrated their right to choose. If they felt a traditional format was more to their standard, then I strongly encouraged them to transfer their child into a traditional school.

Ironically, the traditional places did not work for these individuals, which is truly why they came to PSGL—yet some of them were not willing to embrace our progressive alternative to schooling.

Instead of respecting the fact that PSGL was a school with a distinct mission and design, they made it their business to try to change our program.

As I have already said, this was an easy battle to contend with.

First, all students and staff participated in a community-based intake process. During this time, they received an intimate tour of our program (including our building, our curriculum, and our policies).

They talked with other staff and students to see that our philosophy was alive and well and that it did not rest dormant on paper and was not limited to the preachings of the administrator. Our approach to schooling was very much a part of our culture. It was an element that we took pride in.

Second, when the entire intake process was said and done and individuals still wanted to join our team, they signed an agreement that outlined our program's philosophy and structure. This agreement also outlined our expected code of conduct, associating their signature with their full acceptance of our program.

The third thing we did to promote our nontraditional program and proactively address naysayers was to visit other schools whose philosophy or design was similar to ours. Usually when we went, PSGL would get recognized for our innovation. This was one of my secret weapons of dealing with the unspoken challenge of our unique design.

If there were staff members who had great potential for our school but were paralyzed by traditionalism, I would take them along on the trip. Through this trip, they became more open-minded; it expanded their perspective at a rate greater than if I had sat them down to personally debate the issue.

Finally, we had a school climate that addressed violations to our policies. There were students and staff who were very loyal to the program and did not shy away from addressing toxic behaviors.

Once I received a note from a student who was very concerned with a parent's public display of disrespect for one of our teachers. Interestingly enough, the teacher who was attacked was not a favorite of this student, and I was caught by surprise that she came to this teacher's defense.

I am proud that this student knew not to cross the line to address the parent's behavior. But she did mobilize a group of her peers to sign a letter of concern.

When the matter was presented, the parent immediately accused the teacher of lying. She believed the teacher initiated this campaign for justice. But it was not the teacher who brought the matter to me. It was the students.

Whereas this behavior may have been accepted or tolerated in other schools, it was not accepted at ours. Instead of the "administration" policing our school, our school's climate allowed students and staff to police our school as well.

Through our intake and training process, along with our culture of connected schooling, I was proactive in my approach to tackle the battle of those individuals who believed in only one way to do schooling. I did not have to outline the giant. In this case, I had enough weapons to defeat him whether he was visible or invisible.

The Paradigm and Social Construct of Power

Without looking into the schoolhouse, there is a general concept of power within our society that exists in the abstract realm. Because power is implied, the notion of changing the paradigm and social construct of how power is assigned, shared, and used truly activates a battle.

So if there is a general battle that exists in society when power is redistributed within traditional institutions, one must concede to the fact that PSGL really had to engage in warfare. Because not only was power redistributed, it was redefined inside a structure that others could not identify.

At PSGL, the rules of warfare changed. Now, individuals who had previously been powerless had become valued shareholders to power.

This truly ruffled a lot of feathers.

Power is one's ability to control and to have influence. Whether you come from a place where historically you have had little power or historically you have had a great deal of power, there is a strong paradigm and social construct that maintains our notion of how power is accessed, who has rights to this power, and how it traditionally keeps subgroups in consistent roles of superiority and subordination.

The fact that this delineation, between who has power and who does not, has been passed down over the years, throughout generations, can definitely feed the ideology of who should and who should not have power.

When power has been used a certain way for so long, we establish an unspoken, universal truth around it. Because it is not verbalized but assumed, expected yet implied, it is difficult to challenge.

This battle over the paradigm and social construct of power manifested itself at PSGL in several areas. Teachers came into our program with the unspoken expectation that they controlled power within the classroom. Even well-intended teachers, who wanted to promote student power, still struggled with giving up a little control in order to assign specific power to their students in the classroom.

So when the concept of shared power surfaced, it was twice as difficult to incorporate. If teachers could not assign power, how were they going to share it?

I was able to address this area with two different approaches. First, I took on the role of teacher coach for my staff. And for those teachers who received me as such (I will talk later about the paradigm and social construct challenges of leadership), a strong relationship evolved that allowed us to talk openly and honestly about our assumptions and even prejudices relating to our perceptions of power.

The second thing that I did to address this battle with power was to allow teachers to train their colleagues on how to incorporate and use a new definition of power. This is an area that I am especially proud of with my teachers.

Admittedly, it took some of them longer than others, way longer, to learn how to view power differently. But those teachers who were a match for the program were willing to embrace the notion that the role of power needed to be redefined. And they truly worked at self-reflecting and being self-aware about their perceptions, so that they could fully embrace the real emotional work associated with student empowerment.

And they did it well.

It is important to note that these teachers, who became role models for new teachers and staff, were both Black and White. This ethnic diversity was powerful in that each cultural group wrestled with its own unique version of the battle with paradigms and social constructs.

I talk more about the cultural dynamics to our program when looking at other paradigm battles (later in the chapter). But it was here, where teachers had to face sharing power with students, that we began the discussion of unspoken belief systems and the implied notion of being entitled to power.

I must end this section with an admonishment to my reader to examine your prejudices beyond the classroom.

The battle of the unspoken perceptions of power goes beyond an instructional challenge (where we look at redefining how power is shared with students). While difficult, challenging a teacher on the notion of sharing power with students was easier than challenging a teacher on the toxicity of the stereotypes and prejudices they were unwittingly governed by.

To deal with the struggle one has in sharing power with students, all we simply had to do was to remind people that we were in the business of student empowerment. For individuals who were earnest in their efforts to promote student empowerment, the confrontation merely opened doors for us to deal with the very real, yet secret, hang-ups that one has with giving power to disadvantaged children.

But what happens when you do not have a platform to deal with those secret issues that are deeply embedded in each of us? Even worse, what happens when you believe you have evolved beyond the violators of our past, where people relished and excelled in a space of racism, sexism, or any other ism you can think of?

The truth is, reader, that every last one of us in today's modern society still possesses a toxic thought pattern of prejudice and stereotypes. You see, even when we try really hard to rid ourselves of toxic thinking, I believe we still struggle with toxic remnants that prevent us from participating authentically in a system of redefined power.

Paradigms and social constructs are not easy to destroy. Because there has typically been a historical view of power and even of how the urban and minority communities are perceived, we have to embrace that there is a long, continuous process of dealing with a new idea of defining, accessing, and sharing power.

When we fail to consciously acknowledge the not-so-pretty places within us, we cannot consciously do anything about it.

So while yet unintentional, ignorance prevails, oppression continues, and student empowerment is stifled.

The Paradigm and Social Construct of Leadership (Division of School Power)

The discussion on the battle of power is a great transition into the next two sections, which both relate to leadership.

First, there is a definite paradigm and social construct of school leadership, and generally, it is limited to the concept of administration. Traditionally, the administrative staff is considered to be leaders, and the teachers are not.

Having had more experience on the teacher side of schooling than on the administrative side, it is easy for me to discuss the lack of power and voice that is usually experienced by teachers. As a result, a paradigm develops, making administrators the bad guy and teachers the victim.

However, this paradigm is actually quite funny. I am not suggesting that power is equally shared between teachers and administrators and that teachers do not have a valid argument when they complain about their administrative team.

But what I am saying is that the paradigm and social construct of power is so much of an issue, and the battle over power is not limited to only two players within the world of schooling.

Just as teachers feel powerless with administrators, students feel powerless with teachers. And even more revealing, administrators can feel powerless with the central office (the district), and the central office can feel powerless within state governing structures.

I would not even begin to presume that I could tackle this systemic fallacy of power that is pervasive within our educational structure. But I will say that I worked hard at redefining leadership within my own building so as to eliminate divisions of power. It was really important that power was shared. As a result, power was redistributed.

It was in the redistribution of power that I was able to see the fundamental elements of the battle with leadership and power. And ultimately, I had to face implied ideologies that had a compelling presence when paradigms and social constructs were disrupted.

In our building, there could be no "us" versus "them" construct. And this inability to identify the enemy, the "them," made it very difficult for individuals who had been trained to war against leadership.

And no, there is no official training camp to make teachers so distrusting of administrators. But like any other movement or social phenomenon, it travels by way of simple social interactions.

Visit any teacher's lounge, hang out with teachers after work, or sneak up on a group of teachers who are engaging in a quick chat in between classes. Is it not fair to say that 50 percent of the time, the discussion is going to center on administration (while another 40 percent will center on students and parents)?

So when I hired an experienced teacher, especially one who did not come from a small, alternative-based-schooling model, it was guaranteed that the teacher would bring that mindset into our building.

And here is where the battle existed. At PSGL, I developed a teacher leadership model in which each individual had a voice in both the instructional and operational elements of the school. While work was specialized in specific areas, leadership was not. Power was not top down. It was shared.

If a problem existed with the bathrooms, we did not wait for the person assigned to janitorial duty to resolve it. Many of the teachers would jump in and fix it. They felt that they owned the program, and therefore they took ownership of the problems.

In addition, if there was a problem with meeting some of the instructional objectives among the teachers, it was not uncommon for individuals working in the business office to give their opinion as to the problem or to make some suggestions. The intention of the teacher leadership model was for the school to belong to us as a unit.

But teachers who came from traditional systems had a different mindset about school operations and school instruction. And they would voice their concerns. Usually, they did not voice their concerns within the structure that had been provided for concerns to be addressed. Instead, they discussed their concerns in private, one-on-one encounters.

In the beginning of the program, I did not know how to combat this toxic behavior proactively. I usually had to wait for the problem to surface as a real and tangible issue before I could address it. But by then, time had allowed that toxic entity to take root in our system and impact us on multiple levels.

But as I began to understand all of the paradigms and social constructs, I created a document and system called the Seven Performance Areas.

One of those performance areas was leadership alignment, which included specific leadership expectations assigned to all staff. New teachers were hired with this leadership expectation in mind, and they were trained for it.

This expectation also made its way into the work agreement that was signed between the new employees and me. The expectation became grounds for employment; therefore, violations of leadership alignment also became grounds for termination.

As with student expulsions, I only had to terminate one staff member. The others who had a hard time working side by side with all leadership, instead of being in a position of finger pointing, typically would just leave. If I was not effective in coaching them out, their inability to connect with their peers (beyond complaining) made them feel isolated.

A huge part of teaching is community. At PSGL, our community was based on the shared leadership model. It was not that we did not have problems, but generally, problems were not delineated into an "us" versus "them" battle.

The Paradigm and Social Construct of Leadership (Do Race, Gender, Class Matter?)

Not only was there a battle in how leadership was viewed as relating to school administration, but also in how leadership is viewed in the larger constructs of society.

Whether we want to admit it or not, the images that we see of leadership in the media, in established institutions, or within our social networks, can definitely create a universal concept of leadership in our minds.

So when we encounter those in leadership positions who do not "look the part," it opens the door for us to scrutinize their performance in order to find evidence that would justify our opposition to their leadership.

One of the battles that I am most compelled to fight when looking at empowerment is to scrutinize how we visually define and promote leadership. Students may not understand the technical aspects of leadership. But they can walk away with a visual. We have given students visuals, albeit inadvertently, that communicate to them their future.

I am amazed at the number of schools whose mission is to serve and empower urban Black, Latin, Asian, and even low-income White students, yet do not have these socioeconomic representations on their leadership team.

What is the unwritten curriculum that we teach students? We tell them that they can grow up to be leaders, but we do not employ leaders who look like them?

As a person with an urban, at-risk background, I can say that I never had one African American teacher. And while I was able to pull through and still become an African American teacher, I will admit that I had to struggle with my own perception of Black professionalism.

It was not until I did my internship with Mayor Norquist (Milwaukee's mayor back in the early 1990s) and had the wonderful opportunity to work closely with three of his African American staff, that I could begin to respect the voice and experience of Black leadership.

This is a weird admission and one that has taken me a while to digest. I was raised within an African American family who holds a strong work ethic (thanks to my granny) and is very much proud to be Black. But my experience with positive Black professionals was limited to my family.

There are a number of successful African Americans who grow up with this unfortunate paradigm. As a result, we sometimes have a hard time identifying with the Black community, as our perception of being professional is sometimes challenged by our perception of being Black.

Now, this is not the case for all African Americans, and this is one of the reasons I am drawn to cities like Atlanta, D.C., and even Chicago. Many of my friends in those regions had a different experience than I had and, as a result, did not have to go through a process of detoxing their worldview of Blackness.

As an African American school leader who has a background that is closely identified with the types of students I am trying to empower, I have to be candid, even if I am ultimately judged. I do this so that others can began to discuss the possibility that we have some work to do with the unspoken dimensions of our mission to empower urban students.

There were two other scenarios that I had included in this section that relates to race and leadership in education, but I have deleted them. The issue of "race" is one of those sensitive and controversial topics that I would much rather approach through sound research and not just personal experiences.

However, I will say for this section that I have always embraced the opportunity to serve as both a teacher and a role model for minority students. I believe that part of my work, not only for Black students but for all students, is to represent the profession through the lens or the identity of "being Black."

During my tenure at PSGL, I could not change the world's perspective of the Black experience, but I could take a strong position with my students. As the school's director, I could control the learning environment, and I did so to make sure my students would not grow up with a limited view of their identity.

While the media may present a slanted perspective of Blacks and while there may be a disproportionate number of Blacks on state aid, in jail, and in low-wage occupations, this did not have to be their reality.

So, keeping my eye firmly planted on the prize for student empowerment, I spent my time working with fervency to get students personally connected to empowerment. Every time I possibly could, I took students into meetings with me. I allowed them to see me give presentations, sign contracts, and sometimes engage in difficult negotiations.

After each meeting, we talked. We discussed successful and difficult elements that they witnessed. I even required them to have an opinion, forcing them to put themselves in the position of a leader.

It was important for students to grow up with a different paradigm of leadership. I wanted them to see it from a personal perspective. Leadership is not always a "them"; it can also be an "us."

As they personally identified with me being an urban African American, they grew to identify with me as a leader. When challenges arose from their roles in the service learning program, they often made a connection between what they witnessed and what they believed they had to do.

It was for this reason that I opened myself up to being their role model. Being Black, female, and urban allowed my principalship to impact students in ways that can never be gained through reading a textbook.

I trust that when faced with opportunities of leadership, they will not wrestle with the power of their voice. Like many heirs walking into the dynasty that has been left for them by their parents, I hope I left behind a paradigm for my students to take and pass on to others.

I am not always pleased with the political decisions of President Barack Obama; however, I am excited about his presidency. Having an African American in office allows us to examine paradigms and social constructs of power and leadership that we have not yet been challenged to explore.

The invisible is becoming visible. And even though at times he looks defeated, his tenacity and courage in handling both adversity and victory provides me with the same images of leadership that I tried to provide my students.

Whether we question our unspoken views on the physical perceptions of leadership or our unspoken views on the conceptual assumptions of leadership, President Obama's presidency is outlining the giants.

We will only deal with issues of leadership and race as people of color start assuming more positions of authentic and coveted power.

BATTLE 2: PUBLIC EDUCATION AND SOCIAL CHANGE

Sometimes I find myself questioning the charter school movement. While I am certainly pleased that the opportunity exists, I wonder about the fundamental elements that drive the movement and generate momentum.

Is the charter school movement about redefining instructional genius in the classroom? Is it about redistributing power between the public, the district, and the states? Is it about redefining school leadership, integrating principles of competition and entrepreneurship? Or is it about providing additional educational options for students?

While I am sure we can say yes to each of these questions, we have not found ways to adequately measure these objectives. Without a concrete measurement in which we can agree to the fundamental worth of what is being assessed, the success of the charter school movement is left to a subjective evaluation, leaving its strength open to the interpretation of both supporters and opponents.

Of course as an urban American, a former charter school operator, and a former at-risk learner, I have multiple stakes in the mission of charter schools. Frankly, I am committed to the success of all forms of schooling. Private, charter, choice, alternative, and traditional, I want to see students prepared to live a life of production, prosperity, and promotional growth.

I want students to be empowered to make real changes and improvements in their lives. Some students come from homes and communities where it is ingrained in them how to do this. And I believe these students and those families can serve as our example.

But we know that a significant number of students do not come from this reality. And the next institution available for them to get this training is public education.

Yet I am afraid that public education has become so many things that it is hard to pinpoint the one thing that it does really well.

And until we are willing as a whole to change our paradigm and social construct on public education and social change, I feel that we are going to be throwing ourselves into movements that have great potential but no real changing impact.

I am a fan of charter schools, but I am not an advocate for how charter schools are measured, how they are opened, and how they are closed. While there is a greater level of accountability for charter schools, as there should be, I think our notion of accountability ultimately causes more gaps in the learning process than it does to promote it.

When schools open and close, it has the same impact on learning as do the acts of parents when they move their child from school to school. This mobility has been proven by research to be adversarial to progress, and likewise, opening and closing of schools should be viewed in the same way.

As a charter school operator, I always felt that I had a twofold mission. I had to meet the conditions of my contract, and I had to fulfill the mission of urban empowerment.

While the contract was gracious enough to include outcomes of empowerment in the language, the school was ultimately measured on academic outcomes that did not relate to the true nature of our learners.

I need to be careful in saying this because I am not trying to avoid the responsibility of teaching students core academics. Quite the contrary!

One of the seven tenets of empowerment centers on Personal Assets. It is this tenet that declares the importance of basic skills and strives to promote student proficiency on statewide tests.

But when you are dealing with a population that is deficient not only in their academics but in their spirit as well, it is very difficult to prioritize core academics to the point that you are not able to address other aspects of student development, such as character, identity, ownership, and self-love and respect.

If we really want to make a difference in how students achieve, we need to make a difference in how we are willing to serve them. If our students come from environments where character, self-love, ownership, and identity are taught, we do not need to change the system for them.

But for those students who come to school hungry, sad, scared, and emotionally hopeless, we have to be willing to expand our view of public education.

These students need us to meet them where they are. And schools need the flexibility to go after this objective with support and respect equal to the support and respect we have for increasing standardized test scores.

But if we limit the charter school work to traditional assessment measures, then we are going to end up with the same outcomes.

There is a biblical saying, "You cannot put new wine in old wineskins." This is my belief with the charter school movement. You cannot measure innovation and social change by traditional tests.

I am not saying that we should throw the baby out with the bath water, as I do believe standardized testing has a role that we need to value. But it is not the be-all and end-all.

The be-all and end-all should be in how we equip students to own their achievement. It should be in how we empower them to produce, to prosper, and to promote growth.

Until we find a way to empower all students, even those who come from disadvantaged backgrounds, we are not going to get sustaining results.

Sure, we can get the quantitative results that we want, if we focus on this objective and prioritize it above all else. But I know many people who can read, write, and compute who are helpless, hopeless, and as a result, serve as a weight to this society and not as an asset.

My desire is to impact public education in a way that we can see long-term and meaningful results with our graduates. To do this, we must learn to do more than just school our students. We must learn to empower them.

BATTLE 3: ORGANIZATIONAL DESIGN AND OPERATIONS

We had a tall order to fill at PSGL. While I talk in the previous section about my concern over how we prioritized and defined achievement, I never strayed from my contract's objectives.

Each year, I was determined to get closer to meeting my twofold objective, and I took ownership in how that was to happen.

Ultimately, the limitations on money really impeded our ability to staff for the mission. But I like to think of myself as a problem solver; therefore, I was constantly looking for ways to be resourceful in my mission, in my contract, and to work with the reality that we really did not have the resources to effectively hit the vision.

But I believe we got pretty close. And I believe that the lack of funds along with all the challenges outlined in this chapter really gave me insight as to effective leadership.

Two of my favorite (borrowed) proverbs that we used at the school for empowerment were "Begin to be today what you will be hereafter" and "He who is faithful with a little can be faithful with a lot!" My personal standards of leadership were guided by these proverbs, and I made it my personal mission to achieve and to produce results, no matter the circumstances that were before me.

Instead of spending my energies fighting things I could not change, I focused on what I could change.

In my second year, I had another one of those universal impressions in which I believed I heard the following: "I am going to teach you how to do a perfect work with imperfect people."

I did not need to stop and process what was meant by imperfect people, as I believed all of us—students, staff, parents, the district, the public—are guilty of being imperfect, while at the same time having the responsibility to complete a perfect work.

I think few politics are grounded on malicious intent but very much shaped by the imperfections of people trying to do good.

So, with this as a reality, I focused on the element of "doing a perfect work with imperfect people." And that is when I stumbled on the notion of organizational design.

Once I looked into graduate programs, I discovered that there is a psychology and a business element to organizational development. I wish I could take credit for discovering how an organization's design impacts its productivity, but I rest in the comfort of knowing that I was enlightened to learn this truth even though I did not have a background in business.

Organizationally, there were several elements that impacted us. Our lack of resources, our student population, and the pool of people available for hire all played a part in the strength of our organization.

First, there was the issue of needing to hire teachers who were both certified and knew how to connect to our population of students. Secondly, there was the issue that our school functioned within an open space that promoted the notion of shared power but threatened our efforts to specialize and promote individual accountability.

And finally, there was the fact that we had to contend with all of aspects of politics (as discussed in this chapter) without have a team of people out there to play the game.

We had to find a way to address these challenges. Simply acknowledging them without solving them would have only made us as weak as the problem.

Each year, I worked to solve the problem by strengthening our organization's structure. In year one, I focused on learning the unique needs of our students, our building, and our curriculum. While we always had three instructional blocks in the day, we had to learn how to transition from one period to the next (within the strengths and weaknesses of the building's design), and we had to learn how to discipline in a way that had a schoolwide focus, all the while upholding the standards for empowerment.

In year two, we worked on learning the operational and business demands of the contract. It is one thing to respond to an audit and another thing entirely to be structured for an audit.

Funny—I went in knowing how to organize for instruction. I came out knowing how to organize for business.

In year three, I began to embrace the reality that working at PSGL was a job. While there was a mission that everyone was committed to, that mission alone did not guarantee a professional standard and a professional performance from the employees.

I learned how to strengthen policies to showcase standards and how to police performance. It was very naive of me to think that the mission alone would promote production.

In year four, I revised positions to align with the reality that students needed teachers who could effectively teach them and the contract needed teachers who were certified. These two needs could not be unilaterally addressed with our level of resources.

Ideally, we wanted to hire teachers who were both certified and culturally competent to deal with our population of students. But those teachers were expensive and tended to gravitate toward organizations that could compensate them for their value.

So I redesigned the organization's structure to allow for two types of teaching positions: teachers who were certified and teachers who had cultural competency. The reality is that we could not afford to hire teachers who possessed both.

Year four is when I also instituted a formalized system for weekly supervision that incorporated data along with professional coaching.

Each week, individuals had to list their accomplishments as related to their weekly objectives, and they had to support their achievement with data. If teachers did not produce acceptable data, my lead teacher and I met with them to provide professional support.

Through this weekly supervision, there was a noticeable improvement in the students' achievement. When teachers were evaluated by weekly data, all of a sudden, students started to become more aware of their own achievement data.

This supervision process had a positive impact on the culture of achievement that was in our building. Whereas there had always been an emphasis on achievement, the incorporation of data into year four transitioned the culture of achievement into a more tangible experience.

By the year five, I had an amazing individual who served as the school's lead teacher and I had two powerful advisors who owned the psychosocial achievement of our learners (along with doing the public relations to keep our parents satisfied).

The fifth year was really nice, as this was the pay-off to four years of labor. Because I had designed an organizational structure that truly aligned with both the mission and the dynamic challenges associated with its politics, year five I was finally able to fully step into the role of the executive director.

IN CLOSING . . .

While I think my work with PSGL was about student empowerment, I think it unveiled the politics of empowerment. In order to move forward in this mission, we have to understand the political work and accept that it is just as important as the school's instructional design.

NINE

The Results of Empowerment

Through instructional and organizational programming, the empowerment philosophy and its seven principles combat the experiences of learned helplessness in our community. As a result, the "I can" identity that is necessary for students to access power so that they may produce, prosper, and promote growth is instilled.

This was the work of PSGL. As an agency for social change existing as a public school, our aim was to give students the identity they needed to challenge the notion of "I cannot."

The "I cannot" phenomenon fights against students' natural drive to achieve and generates a perception that power only exists within institutions, ultimately leaving students to feel even more powerless. The end result is an achievement gap in our schools, because students are handicapped in their own ability to produce, prosper, and promote growth.

While we work aggressively as a nation to close the achievement gap, at some point we are going to have to acknowledge that student empowerment must serve as the primary catalyst to generating the much-sought-after results.

Regardless of the amount of accountability sanctions that are levied on teachers, schools, and districts, and regardless of the instructional creativity that is employed in the classroom, we have to activate the spirit and the know-how of "I can" in each learner. Because only through the efforts of each student (as they ultimately hold the key to their own achievement) will we transform the outcomes of America's education system.

The transforming activation of spirit and know-how for each of its students is what constitutes the success of PSGL. As the first runner of the empowerment model, PSGL deconstructed the identity of failure championed (either knowingly or unknowingly) by the students who enrolled in our program. While it did not eradicate generations of learned helplessness within the five years of its existence, it did make a case for a cause and provided a platform for possibilities.

Through the inaugural efforts of PSGL, students were able to outperform their peers in areas of scholarship and leadership. As the developer of the empowerment model, I feel forever grateful to the Milwaukee Public Schools District for allowing the model to make its first appearance. Together, we were able to change lives by instituting the "I can" disposition within our students.

SCHOLARSHIP

At PSGL, every student was a scholar. They were scholars in how we looked at them, in how we talked to them, and in what we expected from them. As a result, students took on the identity of scholarship. This identity along with the empowerment model allows me to talk about scholarship as an outcome and not just as a process.

PSGL students should definitely be recognized for their "I can" academic achievement.

"I Can Do My Work"

A grade point average (GPA) is the average of all your scores for a given grade period, school year, or school career. In order to get a passing or even a decent GPA, students must be successful in fulfilling their responsibilities.

For each year of its existence, PSGL high school students maintained an average GPA over 2.0. Considering that Milwaukee Public Schools for 2009 had an overall GPA of 1.87 among all of its students and an average GPA of 1.73 for the African Americans, PSGL's 2.26 GPA for its Black student population is significant.

To maintain a 2.0 GPA, a student must participate in class, must complete homework, and must successfully participate in unit quizzes and tests. This performance is not so simple for students who suffer from learned helplessness. They typically enter the program with a track record of failing and a minimalist mind-set, meaning that school is a place to attend and not necessarily a place to achieve academically.

Not only should we look at these students in terms of race, but we should also examine their performance from a socioeconomic position. There were seventeen schools that matched our socioeconomic profile. Having an African American population of at least 80 percent and a Free and Reduced Lunch (FRL) status of at least 80 percent, these schools averaged a 1.47 GPA (1.43 for charter high schools and 1.5 for traditional high schools).

The purpose of closely examining high schools with a similar socioeconomic and racial profile is twofold. First, it provides baseline data for comparison. It can be assumed that if our students were at one of these seventeen schools, they would have maintained a 1.47 GPA. Through the "I can" work of the empowerment model, our students took a more serious position with their scholarship responsibilities, outperforming their peers by 79 points.

The second reason why the performance of these seventeen schools is used in this discussion is to highlight issues related to equity and integrity in the assessment process. While we ultimately want students to be able to fully compete with all students (regardless of demographics), we must make room for the varying impact that socioeconomic conditions have on students from different experiences. By making a case for all things being equal, we can better demonstrate the effects of empowerment.

"I Can Take a Test"

Each state in our country has devised a testing system to measure academic achievement in basic core areas such as reading, writing, math, science, and social studies. While many of us will agree that these tests are not a foolproof system for measuring achievement, we will agree that they do provide quantifiable data for us to track performance and as a result make critical decisions about our programs and policies.

Likewise, the empowerment model is certainly more than the core academic areas of reading, writing, math, science, and social studies and in no way should the value or potential of the program be limited to data derived from these standardized scores. However, one can surmise that if students are in fact empowered, one indicator of that empowerment should be visible in test scores.

Such is the case for the empowerment results at PSGL. Through our program, there definitely was a transformation in how students embraced testing. The data showcases the transformative power of empowerment with students who have been disempowered and disengaged within the institution of schooling.

Test Participation: In my years of teaching, I have never seen students excited about test taking. In all fairness, schools have to employ incentives for students to attend school during the testing window. While PSGL functioned like most schools in trying to persuade students to take all portions of the tests, it typically had a higher participation rate than others.

In the 2008–2009 school year, PSGL had a 99 percent test participation rate (100 percent for the middle school grades and 97 percent for the high school grades). The real achievement in test participation is understood when comparing our performance to other schools comparable to ours in demographics. When looking at the seventeen comparable high schools, PSGL had a greater participation rate higher than all but five (one in which PSGL and the school's participation rate tied).

PSGL maintained a 100 percent testing participation rate for middle school for the last three years of the school (with the one exception of a 75 percent participation rate for the reading test in 2007).

In all, PSGL had a greater impact on our students in regard to their attitudes toward testing, which I believe is in part due to how well we promoted the "I can" thinking within the empowerment model.

Test Performance: Now that I have returned to school, I am exposed to current research that truly questions the validity of standardized tests. I am bewildered about how we can continue to use data from these tests to determine academic merit and student performance. Knowing that the intent of standardized test scores is to sort, separate, and rank, why are we surprised when we see achievement gaps between students? Does not the idea of ranking and separation imply the notion of a gap?

But the purpose of this book is not to take on the achievement gap battle. Its purpose is to shed light on empowerment. And these tests can provide us with a window of understanding when looking at empowerment. All things being equal, all players taking the same test, there must be some analytic merit to draw meaningful conclusions.

With this in mind, let us take a look at the performance of PSGL students (98 percent Black) and compare them to other test takers throughout the district and state. It is not far-fetched to conclude that our students were definitely influenced by the distinct nature of empowerment.

In 2009, our high school students were fully competitive with high school students throughout the district. Without isolating students based on their ethnic or socioeconomic background, our African American population outperformed Milwaukee Public School students in all five testing areas: reading, language arts, math, science, and social studies.

PSGL students even outperformed the state. When comparing students based on their ethnic background, PSGL students outperformed their peers at the state level in four of the five areas in 2009 (reading, language arts, science, and social studies) and outperformed their peers in reading and language arts in 2008.

The most significant area of analysis, when examining achievement data from state standardized tests, centers on a socioeconomic comparison. As stated in the previous section, there were seventeen high schools (traditional and charter) that matched our student profile racially and socioeconomically.

Examining the performance of these schools in 2009, PSGL outperformed all of the traditional schools in four out of five areas: reading, language arts, science, and social studies at 86 percent. In 2008, PSGL also outperformed all of the traditional schools in reading, language arts, and science.

Out of the seventeen matching high schools, ten of them were charters. I separated them from the traditional schools in order to provide a stronger comparison to PSGL, which was also a charter.

PSGL students outperformed their peers at all ten of the charter schools in language arts, science, and social studies in 2009 and outperformed their peers at all ten of the schools in language arts and science in 2008. PSGL students also were competitive in the other subject areas in that they outperformed 80 percent of the schools in reading and 90 percent of the schools in math (2009).

While middle school learners were not exposed to the empowerment program to the degree to which high school students were (as relating to time), there is also evidence that the program impacted them as well. In 2009, PSGL's seventh-grade students outperformed 100 percent of traditional middle schools housing students of similar racial and socioeconomic background in both reading and language arts.

In 2008, PSGL's overall proficiency rating for math was 30 percent, exceeding eleven of sixteen schools with similar profiles, and the proficiency rate for reading was 50 percent, which exceeded all sixteen of those schools.

Whether it was in testing participation or testing performance, the "I can" phenomenon of empowerment, fighting against the "I cannot" mind-set of learned helplessness, makes its case.

True, there are areas for improvement. I believe this will be seen when schools specifically serving at-risk learners have equal access to resources and when advocates of these learners are able to increase their political edge in the battle over defining and measuring "achievement."

But in looking at the basic analysis that these tests provide, there is clear evidence that our students outranked their peers in the core academic areas. There is no question—this is due to empowerment.

LEADERSHIP

PSGL's ability to promote leadership is another area of achievement for the empowerment model. While our performance in this area cannot be compared with other schools, as other schools did not define achievement the way that we defined it at PSGL, I would be remiss if I concluded this book without making a case for leadership at our school.

Leadership is a generic umbrella for empowerment's three outcomes: production, prosperity, and promotional growth. By looking at the "I can" disposition for students to promote growth for themselves and to think critically for their local community, PSGL students took their responsibility for leadership seriously.

"I Can Promote Growth"

It is unfortunate when schools limit achievement to state tests, in that there is so much to consider when looking at a student. Value-added growth and behavioral growth are two areas that are not assessed and reported on by state standardized tests. As a result, we do not give room for their full "I can" disposition to shine.

Value-Added Growth: As explained in chapter 5 ("The Power of Direct Instruction"), our students were assessed three or four times a year in reading, language, and math. The purpose of this assessment was to capture achievement that did not register as grade-level mastery.

If a ninth-grade student tested at the fourth-grade level, this student would not meet state proficiency requirements. So when looking at our school's proficiency levels, one has no idea of the amount of academic growth our students actually promoted.

Students only experiencing one year of our empowerment program averaged an annual growth of .36 of a year. Students with two to three years' experience of the empowerment program averaged an annual growth of 1.2 years. Finally, students who experienced four to five years of our empowerment growth averaged an annual growth of 1.33 years.

The seven students who stayed with us all five years enrolled as sixth graders; however, they all were testing below the sixth-grade level for reading. The average grade level performance at the time of their enrollment was 2.5 years. This means that these students had spent seven years in school (including kindergarten) and had only made a 2.5-year gain, resulting in a loss of 3.5 years.

After participating in our program for five years, all seven of the students made gains, averaging 6.1 years. In short, these numbers tell us that these students had an annual growth rate of 1.22 years while at PSGL. While this is good in itself, one must look at the .42 average annual growth rate that they experienced before attending PSGL and acknowledge that a 1.22 annual rate is outstanding!

Behavioral Growth: Milwaukee Public Schools required all of its schools (traditional, charter, and partnership) to participate in a climate survey. The survey provides qualitative data as to the perception that students, teachers, and parents have about the school's rigor, safety, environment, and governance.

In 2008, 100 percent of our students felt safe, felt that the building was neat and well maintained, felt that the school worked to improve behavior when students broke the rules, and felt that PSGL taught students to value, respect, and tolerate the difference of others. Ninety-four percent of the parents agreed with these statements, and teachers supported this belief by rating the environment and its safety at 3.5 on a 4.0 scale.

The empowerment program put students in the position to own their behavior and to take ownership of their school. This ownership was seen in the suspension rate, as well as in the public recognition that the school received.

Fifty percent of the suspensions that occurred at other schools demographically comparable to PSGL were for acts that threatened the physical safety of others. This was not the case at PSGL.

We had very high standards, and when those standards were violated, a suspension process was activated. Although we encouraged a negotiation and bartering system that would ultimately cancel out suspensions, we were not timid about using the suspension process for students who fully earned them. Through SBC programming, we created an environment where students respected the space and safety of others.

Approximately 10 percent to 15 percent of our students were suspended for physical fights (as opposed to 50 percent at other schools), and less than .004 percent were suspended for weapons (as opposed to 1 percent to 3 percent at other schools).

There were only two times we had to call the police (over the five-year period) for weapons. Once a student had a toy gun that looked real, and the second time a parent called the police because her son felt threatened by another student at the bus stop.

I will admit that fights were one of the areas we had to contend with when the school first started. We learned that this was the way students initiated themselves in new environments. But after the first and second year, experienced students learned other ways to deal with conflict.

We never did eliminate fighting from our culture, but we did minimize it significantly. Ironically, when fights did occur, especially when they involved our veteran students, they happened off-campus. Students strategized places to fight so that their behavior would not come back and harm the school's image.

For the most part, students were able to negotiate through their differences so that fights did not occur as frequently as they did in other places. However, it is important to note that these off-campus fights were ways in which students took ownership of their school.

Finally, the success of our empowerment model as relating to behavioral growth can be seen when looking at attendance rates. African American students at the district level had an attendance rate of 78 percent in 2008 and 78 percent in 2009. PSGL's students outperformed these numbers in both years (having an attendance rate of 81 percent in 2008 and 79 percent in 2009).

"I Can Think Critically"

The basis of the empowerment model is to produce, prosper, and promote growth. Achieving in these areas is not the result of rote memorization or directed learning. Instead, students are given authentic situations and settings that they are required to successfully navigate to achieve success.

As already stated, more than 90 percent of our students had leadership positions that required them to think critically in order to be successful. But what was has not been stated is that 100 percent of our students were able to engage in our project-based learning program (levels 1–4), in which they took global issues, explored them for embedded problems, and then developed solutions for the community that were realistic, practical, and valid.

The other thing that has not been stated is that more than 95 percent of our students engaged in the yearly portfolio assessment, in which they had to present a case for their academic achievement to a panel of community assessors. In this presentation, students demonstrated their skills in advanced levels of analysis, autonomous behavior, communication, collaboration, technology, research, and valuing. These are the skills that students take with them into their everyday lives, and these are the skills that will determine how well they are able to navigate throughout life.

Because of our students' ability to use their minds to serve their community, PSGL was asked to speak and train in various public venues: Wisconsin Charter School Association (2004, 2007, and 2008); Milwaukee Public Schools (2007); Edvisions Network (2004, 2005, 2006, and 2008), and the National Charter School Association (paid to attend as a participant in 2007).

The more time students spent in the program, the more successful they became in their ability to engage in higher-order thinking and global problem solving. Whereas 42 percent of new students (of one to two years) were successful with annual projects, seasoned students (of three to four years) had greater success at 59 percent.

The same was the case for the annual leadership assessment. Only 29 percent of beginning students were successful on the leadership assessment, compared to 63 percent of seasoned students. Just as evidenced with the quarterly diagnostic assessments, the longer students were a part of our program, the more empowered they became.

IN CLOSING . . .

While my aim with the school was not limited to the district's definition of academic achievement, I did champion it, as I believed it would only enhance my work with empowerment. So I embraced requirements on test scores, student attendance, student mobility, parental involvement, special education compliance, and school climate. But ultimately, I measured student achievement by empowerment.

At PSGL, our goal was for students to learn how to access power so that they could produce, prosper, and promote growth for themselves and for others. Because in the end, we did not believe test scores and student attendance would put you in the driver's seat. It may give you an advantage to be first in line, but the combined traits of P³ Commitment, Innate Power, Personal Assets, Global Efficacy, Individual Responsibility, Sense of Self, and Shared Accountability will put you behind the steering wheel of a car all gassed up and ready to soar.

At PSGL, student achievement was based on students' growing disposition to drive, as opposed to their unfortunate, but very real, disposition to stay at the back of the line.

Epilogue

A Charge to Urban Educators

By the time this book is published and in the hands of readers, two years will have passed since the closing of Preparatory School for Global Leadership. My experiences since then have continued to both amaze me and impact me in my initial childhood dream of being a change agent.

Even when I look at the simple (but really not so simple) notion of writing this book, there has been much discovery about this desire for change and the push, or really the fight, for the status quo. While I spent five chapters speaking about concrete methods for empowerment and another two chapters addressing the philosophy of empowerment as well as its politics, I believe the true significance to this book is in the personal story.

I understand that a memoir, someone's life experiences, may not seem to have direct value for teachers and school leaders. This is mostly because as teachers, we are hungry for actual tools. We want to use something that works.

Yet when we look at the history of examining what works, at some point we are going to have to face that it is not really in the methods of education. *Empowerment Starts Here* is not just about techniques.

Empowerment is a social construct that understands the learner as a psychosocial being. It is one that embraces the unwritten curriculum in education, the spoken and unspoken values, the spoken and unspoken expectations, and the spoken and unspoken interactions. It is the "unspoken" nature of our work that speaks to the spirit of who we are.

In saying this, I sit here two years after PSGL and question how many educators are willing to be empowered.

How many politicians are willing to embrace the personal dimensions of public education? How many publishers are willing for teachers to tell their individual stories of not only what works, but also the psychological and social strength that is needed to walk in front of all students, not just disadvantaged ones, and become vulnerable to the real impetus to empowerment?

We talk about achievement as if it were a single entity that can be conquered. And to prove the point, we then look at the merits of that achievement by way of quantifiable measurements. But achievement is relative to the definition we use. That definition is predicated on those in power who make such a definition. And all the while, the growth of our students, along with the growth of the adults who care for them, teach them, and stretch them, goes unmentioned.

In saying this, we stay in a didactic place where we play the game of achievement on the front end yet revel in the work that we selflessly, without public recognition, fulfill on the back end.

We have to reverse this phenomenon. No, we do not throw away high standards for achievement. And yes, we must continue to find a way to measure and master this notion of achievement.

But at the same time, we must not forget about the personal side of our work with students. We must not forget about the personal work that is required to be good teachers. We must become empowered ourselves to empower others.

I am finally in school working on my doctorate where I believe my research will center on the psychosocial impacts of education. I am knee-deep in studies surrounding issues such as power, race, and socioeconomic conditions and inequities within education (curriculum, instruction, philosophy, assessment, and accountability).

I am appreciating every case study and every primary source that has been vetted with a "gold seal" to validate the work of the writer. But I believe books like the one you have just read here are needed to illustrate the day-to-day realities of what it means to be an educator, the one who stands in front of children and the one who personally labors with the emotional (yet rewarding) work when no one else is looking.

I end this book with a charge to other educators. The power of my story is not what I experienced but in my ability to take time to write about it and share. The world of education has this unimaginable way of reproducing the status quo. Students need to hear from those of us who are earnestly working against it.

It is their voice, the voice of the teacher whose experiences closely resemble the experiences of the students, that needs to be heard in boardrooms where policies are made, textbooks are published, and standards are prioritized.

To empower the marginalized, we have to get more stories from the marginalized. Some of our greatest educators had to pull themselves up by their bootstraps and fight to get into the educational arena. There is a wisdom in this experience that gives insight on the fundamental challenges associated with the act of receiving, sharing, and using power.

This is what I miss most about being in the classroom: making learning relevant for my learners in a way that goes beyond "culturally responsive teaching." Personally relating to students via instructional crea-tivity took me beyond textbook teaching or even empathetic teaching.

When teachers teach from the experiences that students can relate to, then the real work of tearing down the paradigms and conditions of learned helplessness begins. It is this state in which the students can begin to trust the teacher and themselves.

In knowing this, I send out a charge. There are many of us engaged in the seven principles of empowerment. Whether we are teachers, parents, pastors, or politicians, we are self-empowered. We subscribe to P^3 Com-mitment, Innate Power, Personal Assets, Global Efficacy, Individual Re-sponsibility, Sense of Self, and Shared Accountability. Because we do, we have a proven track record of empowering others.

It is this experience that needs to be heard. Students need your story. The world needs your story. Many times we need to see people we can relate to, who are doing the things that we have yet to do. I pray that *Empowerment Starts Here* starts a movement in the classroom and that it also starts a movement in the literature.

We have to hear from those who represent those we serve. We have to see what empowerment looks like when no one is looking. We have to embrace that empowerment is still empowerment even when it does not represent the status quo.

My childhood dream of saving the world is firmly rooted in educa-tion, but it extends beyond the classroom. I want to empower those who will in turn empower students.

Therefore, "Empowerment starts here" can really be . . . "Empower-ment starts with *you*."

Index

ability-based groupings, 63, 70; at-risk
learners benefited by, 67; Core
Instruction and, 62; older students
grouped with younger students, 63;
Smith's, 69; traditional tracking
system vs., 63
accountability: additional leadership
for, 96; behavior management and,
106; discipline measures and, 91–96;
emotional challenge of, 87–88;
empowerment and, 88; LASSS and
community sharing of, 47; parental
training in, 98–99; proverbs to teach,
90–91; punishment vs., 97;
reflections used for, 91; Shared
Accountability, 18, 18, 18, 30–31, 67,
79, 103; staff training for student, 97;
student, xxix. *See also* P³ Advisory
achievement: closing the achievement
gap in America, 123–124; higher
GPAs, 124–125; leadership as, 127;
limited space for, xxviii; PSGL
middle school, 125, 127; PSGL
students in 2009, 126–127; student
empowerment as, 130–131; test
scores, 125–127. *See also* test
performance
advisory. *See* P³ Advisory
African Americans: false notions
about, 60, 116; GPA at PSGL vs.
Milwaukee Public Schools, 124;
identity and empowerment, 116;
leadership and race, 116–117; media
representation of, 116; poverty and
race, xiii, 36–37, 119; proverbial
quotes by, 90–91; PSGL vs. charter
schools, 127; PSGL vs. Milwaukee
Public Schools, 124, 126; PSGL vs.
traditional schools, 126; in school
leadership, 115–116; as teacher and

principal, 116
assessment: annual state, 76; cultural
and political nature of testing,
74–75; daily behavior, 77; "I can
think critically", 129–130;
incorporating students in, 83–84;
Institute's instructional
programming, 77–78; Institute's
relationship with P³ Commitment,
78; Institute's relationship with
Sense of Self, 78; Institute's
relationship with Shared
Accountability, 79; Knowledge
Block Project Block and Service
Block performance data, 77;
portfolio as demonstrating student
autonomy, xiv, 130; portfolio
assessment, 75–76; quarterly
diagnostic, 76; quarterly scorecard,
77; sharing power of knowledge,
84–85; students as partners in, 73,
74. *See also* student highlights;
teacher shout-outs; test
performance
at-risk learners: ability-based groups
and predictable format of Core
Instruction for, 67; defined, xxi, 60;
empowerment's benefits to, 127;
false notions about, 60; project-
based learning and service learning
for, 56; PSGL engagement of, 55;
service learning for, 43–44; teacher
relationship with, 93–94
attendance rates, 129
autonomy: environment and student,
25; GLC7 format for student, 26, 51;
as personal asset, 14–15; portfolio as
demonstration of, xiv, 130. *See also*
Personal Assets

About the Author

Angela Dye prides herself on being a product of the urban environment and has a background that personally relates to the at-risk learners she serves.

With degrees in education and social science, Angela identifies as being a social change agent. As an author, school leader, and entrepreneur, her career choices have always centered on empowering individuals who have been socially marginalized and politically disenfranchised.

Through lessons grounded in constructivist thinking, global leadership, and personal responsibility, she has developed an instructional process that embraces seven distinct principles of empowerment. Angela is working on her doctorate in education, where she seeks to strengthen this framework while studying the social constructs of academic achievement.

Angela is currently launching a consulting firm to promote student empowerment and to have a transforming impact on urban education at a national level.

CPSIA information can be obtained at www.ICGtesting.com
Printed in the USA
BVOW020310091111

275612BV00004B/2/P